A RIGHT TO BE MERRY

MOTHER MARY FRANCIS, P.C.C.

A RIGHT
TO BE MERRY

IGNATIUS PRESS　　SAN FRANCISCO

Original edition published in 1956
by Sheed and Ward, New York
© 1973, Franciscan Herald Press, Chicago
All rights reserved
Published with ecclesiastical permission
New edition printed by permission

Cover art by Christopher J. Pelicano
Cover design by Riz Boncan Marsella
based on an original drawing by a Poor Clare sister

New edition © 2001, Ignatius Press, San Francisco
All rights reserved
ISBN 978-0-89870-824-0
Library of Congress control number 2001088860
Printed in the United States of America ∞

To His Excellency, Most Reverend Edwin V. Byrne, D.D.

and

Reverend Mother Mary Immaculata
our first abbess and cherished mother

"Our Lord told Margery Kempe, the anchoress of Lynn, that her enclosed life of union with Him gave Him the greatest satisfaction, and it gave her 'as great a right to be merry as any lady in the world'."

AUTHOR'S NOTE

The names of cloistered nuns and postulants used in this book are fictitious. Nothing else is.

CONTENTS

PREFACE

We are hearing and talking a great deal about options these days. So, here are two options for you, and an opportunity to exercise your keen sense of personal autonomy. Make up your own mind. Follow your conscience. Read the following as: (1) a prologue to this reprinting of *A Right to Be Merry*; or, (2) an epilogue to same. But, then, we just knew someone would be dissatisfied with the options allowed. So, all right, go ahead. Read it in the middle of the book. Or, do not read it at all, if you are a conscientious objector to anything that is proposed.

Still Merry

Expertise is what we are after today. Nature has it in the sensitive area of death. She performs it like a Greek drama, with all the dignity of the inevitable freely chosen. Yet she dances it like an innocent child ballerina, spilling out the story with the effortless abandon of pure dedication. Again, she does it as purposefully as Francis of Assisi, who sang because he had nothing left on earth and had found a Father in Heaven. She knows all about the return of spring and what makes that return possible.

And so, for a chapter penance (since we still have chapter and still do penance), each nun and novice was asked last week to go outdoors and take a lesson in dying and resurrection from nature. It was suggested (by which we mean: Go ahead and do it!) that each one take spiritual notes on dying from what God has to say in nature. A few main points were anticipated, such as: dying ungrudgingly, gloriously, gorgeously, gaily. Because this is the way to live. And because somewhere along the theological way of the present wonderful new emphasis on resurrection, some of us seem to have forgotten how one arrives at resurrection. How Christ did. That it was and it is through suffering and death. Odd, how we can miss such an obvious fact as that we have to die before we can rise from the dead.

Since a handful of us started Poor Clare living in an old farmhouse in Roswell in November 1948, an ecumenical council has set itself down in history, even though one could scarcely say that it has settled itself down in history. Reading the luminous council documents, inhaling all the freshness of challenge and positive change which they inspire, it is painful to witness the wrangling and rebellion and disintegration that are assuredly *non sequiturs* of Vatican II's intentions. Yet, there are many ways of dying. And we here in Squash Valley (our present recreational tag for our monastic estate, because squash doth thrive right mightily in the cloister vegetable garden) continue to believe in life and in springtime.

There are thirty-one of us here in Roswell now, besides the five nuns we have dispatched to shore up a monastery in need. And since twenty-two of the thirty-six of us are in their twenties, it would be exceedingly difficult not to believe in springtime. The gentle foundress of our monastery, to whom this book was and is dedicated, has gone before us to set up a new foundation in eternity. And Archbishop Byrne is with her there. Last February, we placed Mother Immaculata in the center niche of our burial vault, beside our first vicaress, she of the two-toned habit (see chapter 11). And new life springs out of the beauty of their dying. Many little customs in our life-style have been changed, because this kind of dying is part of living. No essentials have been changed, because things fundamental do not become obsolescent, though they can be given new expressions.

We are still wearing our religious habits and veils, and we would as soon take off our skin as our Franciscan garb. Hemlines are a dashing four inches from the floor (saves on the mending) and enclosure veils (see chapter 1) are no longer worn. There's a single screen in the parlor instead of a double grille, because screen is just as valid a symbol of our enclosed contemplative life, and is cheaper besides. The priest has been facing us people since our monastery was built, so we can only be delighted that the whole Church is now in accord with us.

Anything else new? How about dialogue and community discussions? Well, we believe that dialogue with

God, with our founders, with one another is essential, and we have never believed any differently. We have a community discussion whenever there is something to discuss. When there is nothing to discuss, we do not have a discussion. We live the simple life.

Ecumenism? A Methodist minister has given us some splendid conferences. A few months ago, eight young ex-drug addicts, none of them Catholic, rang our door-bell and told us that they wanted to play and sing for us. So, they sat on our parlor floor and played and sang; and we sat behind our enclosure screen and sang to them. We loved these sincere young people. And they said to us: "We're home, here!" That made us very happy.

Because the publisher has earnestly pointed out to me that changes in printed text are very expensive to make, I have tried to show myself alert to that reality by broadly outlining here what is the same (everything important) and what is different (many little things) since 1956. Dying is part of living. The sloughing off of outmoded practices belongs to the life process and should not occasion any contempt for the past. After all, we have a present only because we have a past. And we build a future only by living in the present. Leaf-shedding is not an autumnal entity, nor are bare trees a winter totality; both are part of springtime's promise and summer's fruitfulness.

Uprooting is a different matter, an activity to which we do not aspire. We still desire with all our hearts to be loyal daughters of the Church. We look to the Vicar of Christ on earth as our sure guide to rectitude and holiness; and if his title weren't already "our Holy Father", we'd invent it ourselves right now for our personal use. If there is a vocation crisis, the word has not got through to the young girls who ring our doorbell.

It is just after Sext now, and we have chanted our agreement with the psalmist's statement of position: "I have chosen all Your precepts for myself. Every false way I hate." That is both our stance and our goal, which, together with and under the guidance of our Mother the Church, we desire to hold and to attain. And it reminded me, this Office of Sext did, of a recent applicant, twenty years old, with very long hair and a very short skirt, who fired questions at me most of one Saturday afternoon. I shot back a few at her, of course. And when she left, application blanks in her tote bag, she solemnly pronounced: "Say! You're on the level!" I thanked her and told her that we try to be.

One ecumenical council later, we're still merry.

> Mother Mary Francis, P.C.C.
> February 7, 1973
> Feast of St. Colette

ADDENDUM

But now there comes another addition to this expanding preface. For the thing is, we are expanding. Since the foregoing part of this plump preface was written, in 1973, God has called us to come and exercise our right to be merry as His enclosed contemplative nuns in six new foundations. And now the sixth, only just set down, has taken us back to our beginning: back to Chicago. The six founding nuns and I had no train ride this time, since we have now long since hence been riding on the air above the clouds. So, we took to the air again in this blessed year 2000. It was June 22.

June 22 and that "Friday in September" mark great days in the life of St. Clare. She was busy routing from Assisi those whose absence was highly desirable. She saved her monastery, her community, her whole city of Assisi, from destruction through the power of the Blessed Sacrament which, held high in her hands, over invaders, sent them reeling downward and backward and set them running out of the city with Olympic speed. "I will always take care of you", a Voice from the Sacred Host promised Clare. And the seven ensuing centuries have witnessed to His keeping His promise. Now it concerned His keeping His promise toward His loved community in Chicago, which had suffered from the widespread decline in numbers of our times. So, He decided to crown its one-hundred-years-plus of Poor Clare living with a new chapter and a new beginning. Thus it was that on June 22, A.D. 2000, six little pioneers set out with their abbess from Roswell, New Mexico, for Chicago, there to begin Poor Clare life again.

Beginning again is a happy business. We are invited by God to do this every day, each one in his own life. And what would we need for a new monastic beginning?

Once, at recreation years ago here in Roswell, we agreed on what is radically necessary to live our Poor Clare life. Clearly, all declared, what is absolutely required is, and in this order: the Blessed Sacrament, one another, and our breviaries. Helpful adjuncts, of course, are a monastery to house us, dinner at regular intervals of twenty-four hours, and each a monastic cell royally equipped with a bed and its straw sack mattress and a little wood cell stand that in the simple drama of our hidden life performs the several roles of: writing desk, study table, wash stand. And all this embellished with a little cell bench upon which one can, if not exactly recline, sit. A small reading lamp for sturdier souls who do not immediately make for the straw sack after Compline and nightly ablutions. There is a crucifix on the wall, two cell pictures, a cupboard for things personal. And that's it. What more could be desired?

This new beginning, like the other five, was not accompanied by the soft chug-chug of a train such as first bore us to Roswell, but by the whirring of a giant plane on the runway into O'Hare airport. This huge city-within-a-city could have been once again more than a bit overpoweringly strange to cloistered nuns, save that the first garb we saw were the brown habits of Franciscan friars, and the first faces those of our brothers. Dozens of them. The sons of Francis come to welcome the daughters of Clare back home to Chicago. Suddenly O'Hare airport seemed just a homey little reunion hall. And only more so as scores of layfolk—men, women, and children—encircled us to press sheaves of flowers into our arms, to laugh, to weep, to keep up the steady refrain: "The Poor Clares are back."

A large hired (not by us!) van took us to our temporary monastery. And later we were to be taken to investigate the grounds where our permanent monastery will be built, the exact site having been fixed by the burying of several medals at a chosen spot—a definitive act. So, Poor Clare life resumes in Chicago, as we come full circle back whence we came, merry in the remembrance that we are all en route to our final shared destination, the arms of God.

August 28, 2000

1   BEGINNINGS

*And not only concerning ourselves did the most blessed Francis
foretell these things, but also concerning those who were to come
after us.*

—Testament of St. Clare

The evening of November 7, 1948, was a mild one for
Chicago. We did not need the warmth of the choir
mantles we were wearing in the hot glare of Dearborn
Station at 9 P.M., and our long enclosure veils felt suddenly thick and furry. It was four years since the youngest nun in the group of nine setting out for Roswell,
New Mexico, had "seen the world"; and even to those
who have never stopped seeing it, the world must seem a
bit confusing at Dearborn Station.

After the silence of our enclosure, the shouts and the
clangor were deafening. We clung closely to the parents,
aunts, and uncles who had driven us to the station in
a brave little procession of family cars. Then the
Franciscan friars who had come to see us off began to
take familiar shape out of the bright lights and the din,
and we smiled gratefully for the sense of security their
presence gave us.

It was fitting that the friars should be with us. At the invitation of His Excellency, Archbishop Byrne of Santa Fe, we had been appointed by His Eminence Cardinal Stritch to found a new monastery of the Order in Roswell. That meant one more tiny shoot springing out of the seven-hundred-year-old tree which St. Francis had planted the midnight of March 19, 1212, when he invested lovely, eighteen-year-old St. Clare with a gray habit, white cord, and black veil and called her "the first of my Poor Ladies". That night, in the mean little chapel of St. Mary of the Angels, the Order of Poor Clares (as the Poor Ladies were called after the death of St. Clare) was born. St. Francis' eager little band of barefoot friars had crowded into the chapel holding candles and singing, that midnight when Clare eloped from her castle home to become the first daughter of St. Francis and foundress of his Second Order. The friars at Dearborn Station, Chicago, in 1948 carried no candles and they did not sing. Yet the two scenes must surely have had similarities from Heaven's vantage point.

As the protective devotedness of the First Order encircled our little group of pioneers, the faces of Father Leander, Father Nicholas, Father Leopold, and the others became for me the faces of Leo, Giles, Rufino, and those other first companions of St. Francis, back at St. Mary of the Angels just outside Assisi; and Dearborn Station, Chicago, ceased to exist for me. It was reconstructed in the voice of my uncle saying in my ear: "It's time to get aboard, dear." We all came alive again, our mothers with the lunches their love and genius had labored over all that day, our dads and uncles swinging our suitcases, ourselves with the feeling of strangeness taking possession again. Our hearts were turning toward unknown Roswell and unpredictable new beginnings. No one could shatter such a moment with a word. Then Sister Anne dropped her sewing box.

Now the uninitiated might lightly suppose that a sewing box is a thing to be shoved in the bottom of the trunk when one is packing. A nun knows better. Her greatest material treasures are in that box: that very special fine black thread for darning enclosure veils, the just-right weight and just-right-width ribbons for Office books, the sandal needle for which she would brave fire and flood, some serge ravelings to mend her hand-me-down habit with an artistry that would make da Vinci pale. A sewing box is a thing to be clasped to one's heart. That is what Sister Anne was doing, only she dropped it. Strangers watched in fascination as nine Poor Clare nuns darted expertly after these treasures, retrieving the last special-steel-basting-pin just in time to scramble onto the train again and wave unpoetic thimbles and darning eggs in farewell. This was our good-bye to Chicago, where all of us had entered, received the habit, made our vows, and fondly expected to die. It was the beginning of a new chapter in the history of the Order of St. Clare.

It is doubtful whether any of the porters rushing about Dearborn Station that evening knew the life story of the woman whom the voice of God had declared would be "a light illuminating all the world".

The world has been illuminated for more than seven hundred years by the unfailing light that is St. Clare, but the world at large does not know it. Working, studying, writing in the sunlight, we are not inspired to sit down and reflect that if the sun were not there, all these pursuits would be impossible. We do not make lengthy calculations about the number of artificial lights we should have to keep burning all day to give us a sorry substitute for the sunlight. And if the sun does fail to shine some days, we are usually moved only to the extent of feeling vaguely depressed under our electric lights, and alloying with impatience our hope that the sun will soon shine again.

Our Lord said that the children of this world are wiser in their generation than the children of light. That explains why the wicked who walk in darkness have a truer instinct about the location of the universal light switch and the best way to throw it. The world that has been brightened immeasurably by the shining light of St. Clare, and warmed by the Order she founded to minister to the spiritual needs of the world, does little reflecting on the matter. The children of light walk heedless of the source of their light. The children of darkness know better. And when the hour of darkness is at hand in any country, the first act of the powers of evil is invariably to throw the switch. They raze the cloisters. They turn the contemplatives out of their monasteries with loud speeches about the good of the state and about contributing to the social need. No one is deceived very long by such speeches; those who make them, not for a moment. They are only maliciously satisfied that they have in some fashion managed to deal the Church a blow in her most tender spot.

By a strange paradox, the persecutors of religion are always far more spiritual-minded than the common run of humanity. It is a perversion of spirituality, but it is a kind of spiritual vision nonetheless. One has to be very spiritual-minded to grasp the true meaning of the cloistered contemplative vocation, very convinced of the supernatural values to understand its supreme significance for the universal Church. Those who hold the power in Communist-dominated countries have a very comprehensive grasp of it. They understand its significance quite perfectly. If they sometimes draw red herrings of "national churches" across their atheistic paths, they dare not deal even in half-measures with cloisters. We shall grow old and die, waiting for Russia or Red China to set up "national cloisters".

It is only after the enemies of God have thrown the switch that the children of light begin to cry out for their lost brightness. If the exquisite spiritual romance that was the life of St. Clare and St. Francis could be somehow uprooted from history, the redolence of their love for God and men dispelled from the world by a satanic fumigation, all the monasteries of the Order unpeopled and destroyed, something vital would disappear from the life of each porter lugging each heavy suitcase at Dearborn Station in Chicago. A light would go out in the life of each woman who rushed down the broad stairs of Dearborn Station at 9 P.M. on November

7, 1945, and in the life of each man who settled down in the lounge of the train behind the printed screen of his *Chicago Tribune*. Not because all cloistered contemplatives are saints, by any means, but because of the love of God, Who accepts the gift they have made of their lives on behalf of the world and, by His acceptance, ennobles both giver and receiver.

Like the Trappists and Carmelites, the Poor Clares form part of the contemplative vanguard of the Church Militant. Their cloistered Order was not founded to care for the sick or the orphans or the aged, or to lecture to students, or to convert aborigines in the African bush. They do not belong to any class of society, but to society. The Order of Poor Clares was instituted for the whole world and every man, woman, and child in it. Poor Clares are the servants of all.

St. Clare was a woman who seemed born for nothing else but to be cherished by others. Her noble parents, Ortolana and Favorone, doted on this lovely young creature who was their eldest daughter. Her three sisters and two brothers delighted in her rare beauty, her charm, and her goodness. The young bloods of Assisi were willing to resort to anything short of murder to win her hand. No seventeen-year-old girl ever had a more dazzling future spread out before her. But Clare was not satisfied. Her woman's breast held a poet's heart of such capacity that nothing so small as a world could hope to fill it. Fashioned for loving, and nothing else, to be one man's wife was not her fulfillment. So she became the bride of God Himself. To mother one family of children was not enough. So Clare hid herself in a cloister to mother all the world.

When young Francis Bernardone, who was cut after the same pattern as Clare, began to set spirited, quarrelsome Assisi on its ear with his "conversion", Clare caught the first faint rumor of God's Will for her. Assisi had never been able to persevere in despondency for any length of time, but Francis was the liveliest of her lively population. No one was more extravagant, no one sang with gladder abandon, no one laughed and danced and toasted his comrades with such irresistible charm. When this leader of the moneyed young set rode off in the name of high chivalry to take arms under Count Gentile, the whole city cheered him. When he returned in a cloud of silence, they could not understand. God had spoken in the secret chambers of Francis' ardent soul. Francis had listened. And Heaven had begun to trace the first faint letter of "saint" before his name.

Of all the saints of all times, the world has taken none so completely to its heart as St. Francis of Assisi, the little poor man. But Assisi in 1210 was not ripe for a little poor man. When Francis found his songs again, they all told of God's love. When he regained his taste for comradeship, it was not to elaborate banquets that he invited his friends, but to a tryst with Lady Poverty. He became again a familiar figure in the streets of Assisi, but now he was barefoot and robed in a rough tunic belted with a rope. The small fry threw stones at him. The oldsters sneered. Only a few, like Clare and the wealthy and respected Bernard Quintavalle, felt the breath of God upon the city and knew that Francis had not so much gone mad as become suddenly so completely sane that the city was terrified by his sanity.

Those who like to pretend that comfort and ease, pleasure and dollars, add up to happiness got a nasty jolt from this lover of poverty who laughed and sang for sheer joy because he had nothing under the sun but only a Father above it. "Our Father Who art in Heaven", sang out Francis; and the city seemed to be hearing the words for the first time. Gradually, the sneers softened. After a while, no one threw any more stones. And Clare began stealing away from home in the company of her aunt and confidante, Bona Guelfuccio, to talk to this young "Brother Francis", as he had begun to style himself. Nothing is so irresistible as true sanctity, and all Assisi was suffering the impact of Francis' sanctity in 1211. The ones who still derided him were only using their derision as a psychological self-defense of their own padded, wretched mediocrity. The ones who did not deride him were quickly rewarded. Meanness and pettiness began to fall off their souls like scales, and the little barefoot band around Francis steadily increased its numbers as men discovered in glad amazement the spiritual nobility dormant in themselves.

In Clare's heart, already pledged to God but lacking as yet a sense of spiritual direction, a clarion suddenly sounded. And its call returned to Francis' own heart in a long, clear echo. St. Francis recognized in this beautiful, bejeweled girl a kindred spirit. He had made a wild prophecy one day at the ruined old church of San

Damiano just outside Assisi. Up on a kind of makeshift scaffold, his lean brown arms straining under the weight of the stones he was painstakingly resetting in the dilapidated old walls, he suddenly looked up at the blue Umbrian skies and laughed for pure joy. Then he called out to the little knots of peasants and idlers about the place: "Come and help me in the building of this monastery of San Damiano, for in time to come there will dwell therein ladies by whose holy living the Lord will be glorified throughout His holy Church." It was significant that Francis issued this invitation and made this prophecy in the French tongue, for he spoke French only in his moments of highest exultation.

Of all Francis' seemingly extravagant statements, this one would seem eligible for the prize. The man had not then a single follower. Many people still thought he was insane. His father had disinherited him. The source of Francis' next meal was God's secret. Yet he stood there and sang out his graceful phrases about a community of nuns who would live in this tottering old building and fill the whole world with spiritual perfume. He himself must have wondered afterward what in the world he had meant. And no man ever looked less the part of a founder of an Order of enclosed nuns than the laughing little singer on the scaffold leaning against the church of San Damiano.

But in the winter of 1212, Clare came to him, and Francis knew what and whom he had meant that day.

If Francis did not lie easily in the mold of religious founders, Clare in her rustling silks and ropes of pearls, with her golden hair waving about her delicate face, seemed about the least likely of women to be a foundress in the manner of this exuberant young gypsy. But God knew just what He was doing, though men did not.

March of 1212 came and Palm Sunday. St. Francis told Clare the time had come. She and her cousin Pacifica (Aunt Bona had gone to Rome) stole off at night to the chapel of St. Mary of the Angels, where Francis and his friars awaited her. When he had invested St. Clare with a rough tunic and cord like his own and had thrown a black veil over her cropped hair, he took her to the Benedictine convent of San Paolo. It is typical of St. Francis that he stood in the poor chapel of St. Mary of the Angels, with the little golden fires of Clare's shorn hair burning around his feet and her trusting eyes upon him, without the ghost of an idea as to how or where he was to house her permanently. Francis had that supreme trust which can let God do all the planning and then be ready to carry out His plans without any tortured weighing and planning of its own. The world likes to call this kind of trust "imprudence", but only because it is too staggering a virtue to be taken seriously for what it is. Clare had left everything in the world that night, and all she received in return was St. Francis' personal guarantee that as his daughter she would always be entitled to nothing at all. It was enough for her.

In such a way was the Order of Poor Clares born. There followed the expected aftermath of Clare's raging relatives riding upon the Benedictine convent (I have sometimes wondered whether those long-suffering nuns did not pray with touching fervor that Francis would soon find another dwelling for Clare and relieve their ears of the unprayerful cadences of her fulminating kinfolk!), and of her family's redoubled fury when her younger sister, Agnes, sped after her and was as calmly invested and veiled by St. Francis as though this were the customary way to conduct religious ceremonies.

In all these painful episodes, Clare showed how completely her soul was attuned to Francis' soul. She did not try to argue down her relatives. She knew what hot blood ran in the veins of her knightly uncles and cousins (her father had apparently died sometime during these years, as the chroniclers do not mention him again), for it ran in her own. So, when they made a final attempt to seize her, she clung to the altar! When they did drag Agnes away, she knew it was time to ask for a miracle. She got it, promptly. The sixteen-year-old girl suddenly became so heavy that the six furious men could not move her. Uncle Monaldo lifted his arm to strike her, and the arm became paralyzed. God knew His Italian noblemen. It was just the right miracle for them. Terrified half out of their wits, they rode home at a wild gallop, their surprised horses lathered with sweat.

When the dust had settled, St. Francis took Clare and Agnes to the church of San Damiano, which had been given to him and which he and the friars had been making habitable for the young nuns. His extravagant prophecy was fulfilled. As for Clare, her first biographer, the Franciscan friar Thomas of Celano, says it all when he says: "And Clare came to the monastery of San

Damiano, and there she put down the anchor of her soul."

A few years later, when the youngest sister, Beatrice, went to join Clare and Agnes, and when Ortolana herself went to consecrate her widowhood to God in the community at San Damiano, none of Clare's male relatives said a word, though I imagine Uncle Monaldo flexed the muscles in his good arm nervously and assured God that Monaldo was his humble servant!

All this seems like a nostalgic watercolor from a lost past. It is not. For from this little group of barefoot nuns has sprung a vast progeny. The Order of Poor Clares is more vigorous today than ever. When nine of us waved our last good-byes from the train pulling out of the Chicago station in November 1948, we were also waving a filial salute to our Mother, St. Clare of Assisi. That same year a group of nuns from Valleyfield, Canada, had founded a monastery in Tokyo, Japan. The next year, a new foundation was to be made in Los Altos, California. And since our monastery was established in Roswell, other foundations have also been made in Brazil, South America, as well as in Newport News, Virginia; Alexandria, Virginia; Belleville, Illinois; Los Altos Hills, California; Chicago, Illinois; and Eindhoven, Holland. St. Clare wanted the whole world for her mission field, and she still delights to dot the world with her monasteries. The young girls who fill those monasteries are not drawn by a dim, romantic figure from a misty past. They follow a wonderful woman whose seven-hundred-year-old rule is as new and livable today as it was when she wrote it.

God Himself said that St. Clare would be a light illuminating all the world. Our train pulled out of Chicago. Mother Vicaress began assigning us to our places. Sister Anne checked over the contents of her sewing box. Sister Amata poked about among the boxes which had been thrust into our arms at the last minute and suddenly gave a muffled shriek: "Heavens, someone gave us a case of beer!" Sister Paula found her breviary and began to lead the Litany of the Saints, the rest of us responding. When we came to "*Sancta Mater Clara, ora pro nobis*"—"Holy Mother Saint Clare, pray for us"—we all asked her to fill Roswell with the light of her love.

2 AS PILGRIMS

The sisters shall not appropriate anything to themselves, neither a house nor a place nor anything, (but be) as strangers and pilgrims in this world.

—RULE OF ST. CLARE

With a Poor Clare vocation comes a rare talent for sleep. Where others might find a straw sack laid on boards a thing unbearable, the Poor Clare finds it highly satisfactory. Compline and night prayers are usually finished by 8 P.M. The retiring bell rings at 8:30. Some of our most gifted sleepers would like to abolish that retiring bell; it wakes them up.

I had heard people complain about the impossibility of sleeping on a train, but had not supposed I would ever have a chance to see how a cloistered nun would make out. After all, your solitary chance for a train ride, once you have made perpetual vows in the Order, is to be chosen to go on a new foundation. Scarcely any "foundress" survives to be a member of a second foundation, so I have had my first and last train ride as a Poor Clare. It was wonderful.

Sister Anne and I were billeted together in an upper

berth. With her fine logic, Mother Vicaress had assigned berths by age and girth. "Young, thin ones, up; older, stouter ones, down." Sister Anne and I climbed up and sank into the unfamiliar luxury of a soft bed. We talked for a few minutes just to indulge in the wild extravagance of hearing our own voices after Compline. Mother Abbess, who had preceded us to Roswell with the Novice Mistress, had said we were not bound to our monastic silence on the train, and we meant to take advantage of this. But Sister Anne and I were sleepy. The novelty of being permitted to talk freely did not stand up well against the prospect of sleep. We fell asleep and woke up, from force of habit, at 12:30 A.M. But no one rang any bell for the night Office. No bare or sandaled feet of the "early birds" went scudding past our pullman "cell". We remembered where we were, grinned sleepily at each other, and fell once more into that deep coma which is a Poor Clare's form of sleep. We were still in the coma when I heard Mother Vicaress telling me to "Hurry! Come down! We are pulling into Kansas City."

We had a forty-five-minute stopover there, and I had been given permission to step off the train with Mother Vicaress and visit with my family who lived there. My sister and her husband had driven up from St. Louis with their brand-new baby to share in this unusual visit. In no time at all, Mother Vicaress and I were enveloped in our mantles and long enclosure veils, ready to brave another railway station. This was a fatal strategic error on our part. Cloistered nuns lose the knack of making their way through crowds, because they never see any crowds.

They become very inexpert at finding one certain face in a sea of faces, because any faces they happen to see from the enclosure are set solidly on shoulders outside the parlor grille and are never swimming about in masses of humanity. Mother Vicaress and I must have looked a forlorn little pair indeed, for a kind-faced lady bore down upon us with, "Sisters, isn't there *something* I can do to help you?" There was, but while Mother Vicaress was asking this good Samaritan to telephone my family, my sister found us. The rest of my efficient family was on the train, happily visiting with the *other* nuns. If only we had just pursued our usual vocational course of staying where we were!

My brother-in-law had boarded another car, searching for me. We looked up just in time to see him, the small bundle of baby in his arms, pulling out of the station! I have never been initiated into the mysteries of why train cars slide in and out of stations in the bewildering way they do, as though they cannot make up their mechanical minds which way to go. The memory of that little pink blanket full of my niece, pulling *out*, still disconcerts my memory. "My baby!" shrieked my sister. Altogether, I reflected, visiting at the parlor grille has its points.

Yet it was wonderful, that great privilege which gave me joys I would never otherwise have known again on earth—to embrace each dear one once more, and to hold in my arms for a beautiful minute my tiny, blue-eyed niece. This young person, however, was singularly unimpressed by either my exclaustration or the foundation. It was just a way of filling in time between formula feedings to her, and she slept placidly on (which may be an indication of a future Poor Clare vocation). I knew her eyes were blue because she opened them just once— to look at her father, not at me. When the fleeting minutes were gone, we reboarded the train, caught up with our Office, and prepared to do what sightseeing we could through the train window.

Friends asked us afterward if we kept the curtains down on the train. This struck us as immensely funny. Why should we? When St. Clare sent her Sisters out of the monastery for any reason, she would remind them to praise God for every flowering tree they saw, to exult in every little blade of grass. We were all exclaustrated to make a new foundation. And the thought of doing this in the gloom of a curtained compartment, staring at one another or perhaps at the floor, amused us as much as do the tales of our digging our own graves and sleeping in coffins. What a jolly life! For that matter, though, I suppose a satin-cushioned coffin would be more comfortable than a straw sack. And Poor Clares can sleep on or in practically anything. In my more practical moments, I have often felt genuinely grateful that we do not go all-out for digging graves. I am not much of a hand with a shovel and should probably never be able to provide myself with anything better than a shallow ditch.

To return to the train ride, when a cloistered nun is out of her cloister, she is still a cloistered nun. She observes the spirit of her vow of enclosure wherever she is and as many of its practical regulations as she can when she is outside. Thus, no contemplative nun would wander about the train "making friends" or striking up chance conversations. Neither would she stare about curiously at everything and everybody within her visual or aural focus. No more would an active religious do those things! However, it is certainly opposed to the spirit of enclosure, the hiddenness and obscurity which a contemplative nun professes to love, to call everyone's attention to herself by the singularity of her behavior. That is why our holy Rule and Constitution legislate on this point with expected Franciscan simplicity: "We will that, whenever it comes to pass that one or more Sisters are transferred in this manner [i.e., for the establishment of another monastery], they be accompanied by persons who are trustworthy and above reproach, and that they make haste to arrive as quickly as possible at the convent of their Order assigned to them; and that the Sisters, while they are in the world, shun all indiscreet conversation as well as vain and unguarded looks in respect of any persons whatever; but let them be *always modest and humble, speaking courteously to all, as is becoming.*"

Employing the monastic signs we would use in our cloister instead of speech would be to attract attention to ourselves outside. Sitting in a darkened compartment, shuttering our souls against the acts of love and praise of God which the rolling hills and spreading fields inspired us to make as our train sped past them could scarcely be called an exercise of the vow of enclosure. In fact, I can imagine few things more absurd than thinking we should

not look at God's beautiful countryside. God never yet
made a tree or a flower that would contaminate the eyes
of His contemplatives.

We did not much avail ourselves of the extraordinary
permission to talk. Our hearts were too full of the high
romance of this new beginning, and our thoughts had
already arrived in Roswell. We looked at the scenery
and prayed and dreamed. And then I fell asleep on Sister
Anne's shoulder. The day passed quickly, and we settled
down for a second night on the train. Morning would
mean Roswell.

Everyone was awake betimes that morning, eager for
the first glimpse of New Mexico and impatient to see
our beloved Mother Abbess and the Novice Mistress,
who had been in Roswell since August, working, planning, supervising alterations and additions on the big
white farmhouse on the outskirts of Roswell which was
shortly to become a monastery. Reverend Mother had
written many letters to us about the sunlit warmth of
Roswell in October and November. Our nuns in Chicago had urged us not to bother packing woolen blankets and shawls we would never need in hot Roswell.
Reverend Mother had also written that we could see the
white farmhouse before the train pulled in if we watched
carefully. We dutifully pasted our faces against the train
window, but we could not see our future monastery.
The train windows were covered with ice. Roswell welcomed us with its first frost of the season.

Somewhat shaken, we turned back from the window
to the immediate problems concerned with getting

ourselves and our curious baggage off the train. Sister
Paula dragged the case of beer from under the seats and
giggled, looking speculatively at Mother Vicaress. Would
that resourceful person come up with something plau-
sible for the porter who must carry it out? Sister Teresa
complained bitterly about the way they plastered com-
partments with mirrors so that you could not look anywhere but out the window without seeing your own
face. After fifteen years of not seeing her face, she could
not readjust to it now. Sister Agnes inquired hopefully
whether anyone would like half a head of lettuce. One of
our more ingenious mothers had included heads of lettuce packed in wet cloths in the train lunch she provided.
We were fasting, hoping to receive Holy Communion at
the church before going to the monastery, so everyone
had a decent excuse for not taking on the orphan half-
head, which had not improved with the train ride. I was
just begging Sister Anne to get a really good grip on her
sewing box when the train slid to a stop and we crowded
to the fore to fill our eyes with the two small and very
dear figures who stood shivering on the platform.

Anyone who supposes that a life of asceticism, penance, and silence drains the tenderness out of a religious
should make it a point to be on hand when cloistered
nuns who have been temporarily parted from their spiritual Mother see her again. We embraced her and the
Novice Mistress until their bones could take no more.
We laughed and we cried and then we laughed some
more. We would have sung had the surroundings been
more propitious.

The affection which a cloistered nun comes to feel for the abbess who received her as a breathless postulant clicking her high-heeled way into the enclosure for the first time, who invested her with the gray habit and white veil of a novice and then placed her own firm, warm hands under the trembling young ones when she received her vows, who cared for her needs and guided her across obstacles and quite unmistakably loved her— even in her worst moments!—is a thing as deep and tender as it is sacred. A Mother Abbess worthy of her name is a perfect blend of mother and abbess. In hours of personal suffering or where there is need of small, delicate attentions, she is predominantly mother. In matters of community observance and discipline, she is all abbess. Yet, in the ordinary business of religious living, she so perfectly combines these two functions of her office that the line of separation is completely and beautifully blurred. That is why the love of the nuns for their mother is fortified and purified by a restraining reverence, and why their respect for their abbess is conditioned and sweetened by love.

Reverend Mother had already made some good friends in Roswell, and several cars were lined up to receive her little pioneer community. The cars took us to the Franciscan church, where we received Holy Communion for the first time in Roswell. Now we were at home indeed. After our thanksgiving, we settled ourselves in the cars again, this time for our last ride, to the new monastery.

The old white farmhouse must have thrown out its

frame chest to the utmost limit that morning, for we caught our breath and solemnly agreed it was the most beautiful place we had ever seen. Actually, it was and is just a very plain white frame building with a roguish red roof. An old-fashioned porch runs across the front and half of one side. The roof leaks when it rains, and nothing will prevail upon some of the windows to let themselves be opened. But love transfigures everything, and we were very rich in love that morning. Even to less prejudiced eyes than ours, the ring of tall elm trees encircling the building like an enclosure wall of God's own construction could not seem anything but utterly lovely. There were lilac bushes in the back and broad lawns, still green in November, in front. Tall *arbores vitae* stood in stately pairs at the entrances. And if the whole place lacked that austere façade featured by the ancient monasteries, a broad white signboard at the curve of the drive declared in unequivocal black letters that this was the MONASTERY OF THE POOR CLARES.

The little church of San Damiano outside Assisi would never have dared aspire to be a monastery, but it became one by the mere fact of St. Clare's taking up residence there. It is monastic life which signifies a monastery, and the fact has no vice versa. The most "correct" monastic building in the world would not be a monastery if monastic life did not pulse within it. When Mother Abbess led us to the choir, the first place in the building we saw, she motioned me to open the organ. We sang the *Salve, Regina* in thanksgiving, in humility, in Franciscan joy over a new Franciscan beginning. And at that precise moment, the old white building ceased to be a farm-house and became a monastery.

We sing that *Salve, Regina* each day of the year except on Good Friday: first, because our Blessed Mother is Queen of the Franciscan Order and Queen of our mon-astery and we like to tell her so; and secondly, in union with our beloved Trappist monks, in gratitude for all they have done for us and all that they mean to us. Their way of life is so essentially the same as our own that the bond we feel with the Trappists is forged by something far more radical than gratitude alone. We were forcefully reminded of this when we read Father Louis Merton's *Sign of Jonas* in the refectory. The days follow the same pattern; even the interruptions are the same. All the joys, the sorrows, the work, the prayer as described by Father Louis are ours. We feel that the Trappists are our own, and the beautiful charity extended to our new beginning by the Trappist monks in Pecos, New Mexico, will be perpetuated in our daily singing of their own *Salve, Regina*.

After that first salute to our Lady in the new monas-tery, we released ourselves from the strange rub of stock-ings and leather "going-out-sandals" and ran through the big house like excited children. A former postulant in the Chicago monastery, obliged to leave because of ill health, had arranged all our cells as only one of the initiate could; and the little signs were swinging above each white door: Sancta Anna, Sancta Amata, Sancta Teresa, etc. Often the big white house rang with the new inhabitants' laughter. For, after years of routine work and order in the big Chicago monastery, everything was suddenly fantastically out of line. We were glad that our rule of silence does not forbid laughter. The whole monastery was spotless, because Reverend Mother and the Novice Mistress, assisted by the teaching Sisters in Roswell and the former postulant, had made it so. We later learned that Mother Abbess and the Mistress had still been on their knees scrubbing when midnight struck the night before our arrival. But cleanliness is one thing, and habit is another!

Nuns have such a genius for systematizing things that modern efficiency experts could sit at their feet to learn from the least of them. They have a time for everything, a place for everything, a way of doing everything that comes to seem like part of the deposit of faith. Now, of a sudden, there was no place for anything! We trudged out of the choir after holy Mass to replace our mantles in the cupboard. But there was no cupboard. We washed the dinner dishes and sent them out to the novices to put away. But there were no novices, nor was there any specified place to put specific dishes.

This was all very confusing, but it had something vital to do with our joy those first months. When you come to a mere shell of a monastery and are obliged to start from almost nothing, you have unique joys and fall heir to something of the gaiety that characterized St. Francis and his first friars, St. Clare and her first daughters. Rubbing shoulders all day in the little monastery, packed into the tiny choir, moving from makeshift to makeshift, we began to feel "at home" in the deeply Franciscan sense of the term.

A small passage between the kitchen and the community room, the breakfast niche of the former occupants of the house, became our monastic refectory. In order for the procession to enter this dining hall, it was necessary that one table be moved out of the path. This feat was repeated when the procession departed after dinner and collation. Two nuns would solemnly rise at the appointed time, hoist the table up and back, and then flatten themselves against the wall, not exhaling until the procession had swept majestically out or in. Somehow this never seemed ludicrous. We were happy, but reflective, too. For we had come into our Franciscan heritage. We were not too far from the golden days of the Franciscan Order when St. Francis had assigned each friar his place at Rivo Torto by the simple expedient of a chalk mark down the wall. If we had known theoretically before that the less material baggage one carries through life, the freer and gladder one is, we knew it experimentally that first year in Roswell. We had very little of anything but love and joy. And we needed little else.

Once, during the first community Retreat in May 1949, we had nothing in the monastery to eat except rice and some onions. Mother Abbess pointed out in a pleased voice that the combination was a very good one, and we all agreed. When she explained to the Retreat Master why the menu we provided for him was so chastely unadorned, he grew very anxious—about us, not himself—and spread the word around Roswell. In no time at all, we had armloads of supplies from the good people of Roswell and the devoted nursing Sisters at the hospital. That is how things have always gone for us. We have learned the singing joy of having nothing "laid up in barns, and behold! our Heavenly Father feedeth us!"

If God does all this, we thought, we can labor and spin for ourselves instead of copying the fashion modes of the lilies of the field, who are too splendidly garbed to be authentic Poor Clares in any case. In fact, we labored and darned (our substitute for spinning) so perseveringly, so enthusiastically coaxing old garments to go along with us another mile, that Sister Paula distinguished herself by having her habit literally fall off her once. She had darned and patched that long-suffering robe until its exposed serge nerves could no longer bear the thrust of a needle. One day, the back of it turned down like a secret panel in a wall.

It is not easy to explain the joys of "traveling light" through life, but anyone who has experienced them will never consent to take on excess earthly baggage again. It even simplifies death, for this material liberty carries over unfailingly to the spirit.

The first spring in Roswell, while we were working in the garden one day, most of us stoking fires of the huge tumbleweeds that were rolling crazily around the big field, and Mother Abbess laughing weakly at the youngest Sister, who had failed to recognize the mighty monsters in their infant stage and was enthusiastically planting a border of those "lovely little shrubs" around the lawn, an alarm came. Another Sister rushed out from the monastery with the news that official warnings had come over the telephone that a tornado was bearing down on Roswell. All should get into storm cellars without delay. We had one midget-sized cellar, which would hold limited amounts of turnips and carrots but not a community of nuns. So Mother Abbess lit the candles on the altar, and we all changed our garden veils to go to a better storm shelter and prepare for possible death. Sister Teresa tore up to her cell and returned in about three minutes flat. "I packed", she beamed to Mother. By that terse statement, Sister M. Teresa, Poor Clare nun, meant that she was now wearing her Sunday veil, her "good" habit, and was clutching the relics of saints she had amassed through the years. Her only important earthly possessions were packed and walking around on her. She went into the choir with the rest of us to sing: "*Sub tuum praesidium confugimus, Sancta Dei Genitrix*"—"We fly to thy protection, O Holy Mother of God"—to pray the Rosary, and to wait to be blown up to the Lord. But the tornado was evidently disgusted with our unconcern and took a sharp turn away from Roswell.

People began calling on the telephone to thank us for having averted the tornado from Roswell with our prayers! We thanked God, "unpacked", and returned to the garden. Life is so very simple when we do not complicate it. And Sister Paula remarked at recreation in the evening how it was "so nice" that the tornado did not kill us after all, as Sister Catherine's mother had given us some shrimp and it would have been a dreadful shame for a rare treat like that to be blown into Texas, where people probably had shrimp any old day.

When you come to a makeshift monastery, every little monastic detail that is added to the house seems epochal. Each new little convenience is cause for wholesale rejoicing. When we finally got a mantle cupboard, we almost stood in awe of it. When we could afford some cupboards for the dishes, we were hushed with wonder. And when at last we built a refectory, we almost missed having no calisthenics to perform. Small beginnings are indeed golden days, and that is why we do not aspire ever to grow big.

Those first recreations, Mother Abbess used to regale us with the strange things she and the Novice Mistress had encountered in their sallyings-forth into the world after forty-some years behind enclosure walls in Chicago. A kind gentleman in Roswell had paid their plane fare to Santa Fe to confer with Archbishop Byrne on important details of the foundation, and we congratulated them on having extended their exclaustration to the skies. Mother Abbess insisted that the big plane seemed to them not a whit more thrillingly "modern" than the bus. We went weak with laughter as they described how they had boarded their first bus in Roswell, nodded respectfully to the bus driver, glanced interestedly at the box at his side with such strange slits at the top, and seated themselves to begin a quiet decade of the Franciscan Crown. Surely the two Poor Clares were distinct anachronisms to the driver, but he gallantly refused to smile. Neither did that prince among men comment when the lately exclaustrated Clares held a whispered conference over the curious fact of no one's coming

around to take up fares and the equally odd phenom-
enon of strange business transactions at the "box", with
Mother Abbess at length instructing her companion to
present the driver with a quarter. He obligingly changed
it into two dimes and a nickel, but one doubts that he
was prepared for his Poor Clare fare to beam on him
with a joyous "Oh, thank you! God bless you", pocket
the change, and return to her abbess with the glad news
of what a kingly race was sitting on the chairs of buses in
these latter years.

They related their happy adventure to the Franciscan
friars, and only then discovered the truth when great
barks of masculine laughter broke over their ears. The
incident seems to have become part of the Franciscan
legend, a kind of minor addition to the *Fioretti*. When
Father Provincial came for his first visit to us, the friars
had scarcely completed the introductions at the parlor
grille when they queried: "Does he know about the
bus?"

Mother Abbess and the Mistress had lived with the
Franciscan hospital Sisters in Roswell during the months
before we came, receiving from them the full measure of
Franciscan hospitality and charity. It was while there that
Mother Abbess received from the Chicago monastery a
telegram which read: "Hose and fire equipment on the
way." However well we knew the loving generosity of
our nuns in the monastery we were leaving, no one had
expected them to provide us with the essentials for setting up a filling station. And it was only when huge
moving vans pulled into Roswell and began to disgorge

only such familiar objects as straw sacks, Stations of the Cross, and double boilers, yielding up no gasoline tanks or tire jacks, that the Roswell Poor Clares relaxed. It developed that the abbess in Chicago had actually sent the innocent monastic message: "Whole and entire equipment on the way!"

They told us, too, of the picturesque means God had chosen to manifest His preference about a location for the new monastery. With six sites under consideration, Mother Abbess and the Mistress were leaning toward the big white farmhouse just outside Roswell's city limits and had intimated as much to a new friend in the city who made signs. Mother Abbess was still, however, conferring with the Holy Spirit and wishing He would point a direct arrow at one site—when He did! The next time the two pioneers rode out to inspect the big white house, there was a sign at the turn of the driveway. "Monastery of the Poor Clares" it read, no matter how many times they blinked unbelievingly at it. They bought the "monastery".

Some might attribute this to an old sign-maker's deafness. We credit it to the acute hearing of the Holy Spirit when two Poor Clares asked Him where to establish their new monastery.

They had endless tales to tell us, some uproariously comic, some tender and touching, so that the recreation hour seemed always far too short. Best of all, Reverend Mother told us much of our new spiritual father, Most Reverend Edwin V. Byrne, Archbishop of Santa Fe, who had so graciously invited us to found another house of contemplative prayer in his ancient and historic see, who had welcomed them so warmly to New Mexico. He himself supervised the purchase of our property and showed a sincere and loving interest in each detail of our new beginning. We felt we knew him already. And when he came from Santa Fe on November 12, the eve of the dedication of the new monastery, and entered our community room, we knew we had a true father in our new superior. His tall frame filled the doorway so that the room and the monastery itself seemed dominated by his presence. Then he spread both arms out in a full-length gesture that seemed to gather us all to his heart. We keep the warm memory of his first words to us: "Welcome, my dear Poor Clares." We felt welcomed indeed, and loved and protected. And we knew why the masters of the interior life have said that the spiritual stature of a pastor engaged in active work for souls can be computed by his regard for contemplation. We were pleased that our Archbishop stood so tall.

3 WALLS AROUND THE WORLD

Let the Sisters be most sedulously on their guard lest they be seen by those who enter.

—RULE OF ST. CLARE

"Whassa matter, Sister? You mad?"

No, I was not mad. I was acutely embarrassed. Although we had been in Roswell for three months, it was only on yesterday's graying February afternoon that the strict enclosure had been fully enforced. We had been observing enclosure of our grounds, of course, from the beginning, but construction had continued in full swing. There had been a week of open house, authorized by Cardinal Stritch and Archbishop Byrne, so that Roswellites could become acquainted with the details and the look of a cloistered community, which was entirely novel to them. Many minor prescriptions of our strict enclosure had necessarily been temporarily waived by higher superiors. But now the old farmhouse on the outskirts of Roswell had been stretched, pulled, and pummeled into a reasonably accurate facsimile of a monastery. The workmen had stopped hammering, the last nun had fallen off the last ladder and put her paintbrush away, and Archbishop Byrne had set the bounds of the nuns' enclosure. It was all climaxed with a moving little ceremony that would very likely have baffled most persons. We donned our choir mantles in the intimacy of that February twilight and followed in procession after our abbess, singing the *Te Deum* as she led us from one entrance to another, solemnly locking each from a great ring of keys.

Many a woman would not feel impelled to sing because she was locking herself into a restricted area forever. We did. And recreation that night was very gay. This morning, Mother Abbess had given us an exhortation on the full regulations of enclosure, which had necessarily been suspended during the past three months. Henceforward, if any workman had to be admitted into the enclosure, the portress would accompany him, and the bell would be rung to caution the nuns to remain out of sight. Well exhorted, we went happily to our chores. My first one was airing blankets, and I was feeling pleased with the world in general as I sang softly to myself in that clean February wind and drew colored arcs of blankets over the triple lines.

I heard not a tinkle of the portress' bell, only suddenly, very suddenly, a cheerful masculine voice. "Hi, Sister!" I pulled our veil down, wondering where the portress was (she had gone to get his tools) and what St. Clare would do at a moment like this. She had scattered the Saracens with the Blessed Sacrament and a prayer, but I could scarcely ask her to scatter this one friendly Spanish workman. I said nothing. So now I had a puzzled workman. "Whassa matter, Sister!" His thoughts beat as loudly against my ears as I only wished mine could have beat against his: This is the same young nun who has been painting and hammering and emptying garbage around here since January, the same one who took my wife and children all through the monastery during the open-house week, the one who played the organ at the dedication Mass when we all knelt in the chapel. She always smiled before. "You mad?"

Charity and common sense rescued me at the same moment that the portress reappeared. I smiled. "Of course not", I said. "God bless you." And I disappeared in an inglorious cloud of green and red blankets.

Enclosure baffles so many people. Even those who love and admire the contemplative life think that the importance of enclosure is exaggerated. That is why it must be understood, from the beginning.

What sort of girl elects to narrow the outer compass of her life to three or four walled-in acres? The neurotic? The lovelorn and disappointed? The selfish and shiftless? The social misfit? Such notions find easy quarter in many minds, but it needs only a little common sense to reveal them all as preposterous. Just fancy twenty-five neurotic women rubbing shoulders all the days of all their lives in a cloister. The place would blow up! And the insurance agency could write it up as "spontaneous combustion". A healthy set of nerves is indispensable in the cloister; and by that I mean here: a sane outlook on life, a talent for keeping things in proper perspective, an ability to rise to the unexpected situation and to be content with the expected.

I was sixteen when I knew I had to be a Sister. I was twenty when I realized God wanted me in the cloister. When I went to the Jesuit Father who was then librarian at the university where I was a student and told him I thought I should be a contemplative, I looked into the sunken, wise eyes in his ascetic face and waited for him to tell me something of the penances of the cloister. Maybe I even expected this priest, who had reached my heart in his retreat discourses by the burning mysticism that licked at all his words like little flames, to congratulate me on desiring so lofty a life. At any rate, I was certainly not prepared for what he did say.

"Ever have visions?" Father inquired pleasantly. I started, I blinked, I swallowed, "Why, n—no", I gasped. "Oh. Have you had any revelations from our Lord?" I was now completely taken aback and felt I was revealing the whole of my drab ordinariness when I looked into Father's searching eyes and gave him a second, even smaller: "No, Father." Again I heard that disconcerting, ambiguous reply: "Oh." "Any messages from our Lady?" he asked me. I felt this must be his last faint hope and knew that I could not fulfill it. I sat there miserably, stunned to hear this priest questioning me about mystical phenomena as casually as he might have inquired for the health of my great-aunt Hortense, and realizing all too vividly how completely uninteresting a person I was. Still, there was no good in evading the issue, even if I did not belong in a cloister, even if my most shining dream was disappearing behind a fatal cloud. I heard my own voice revealing my nondescriptness with painful accuracy.

"No, Father. I am a very ordinary person. I want to enter the cloister because I think God is asking me. I like to dance and I like to sing. I love people and love this university. I like books and I'd like to teach. And I would not give up any one of these things for anything less than God." I added the tragic truth again. "But I never had any visions." I stopped breathing for what seemed like a long time and then watched, fascinated, as little laughter lines began to tangent out from Father's eyes. "Good", he said. And he laughed. After a minute, I laughed, too, like a man getting his reprieve on the edge of the gallows.

Father did not expatiate on his comment, but picked up a middle-sized book from his desk. "Put that on your head," he said, "and let me see you walk around the room a few times." Dumbfounded, I obeyed. Somehow (thanks be to God for my love of dancing!), the book did not slide off; and I stood silent before this saintly madman, wondering what he would think of next. He looked pleased and motioned me to a chair. I removed the book and sat tensely on the edge of the chair. His smile vanished. "You'll never make a contemplative if you sit like that. Contemplatives are God's lambs. They frisk on the mountain. They radiate love. You'd frighten anyone with your rigidity. Relax." I did, and Father began to outline the qualities requisite for a contemplative vocation. He spoke at length of a love for silence and interior prayer. He spoke at equal length of a sense of humor. And each unfolding year of my life impresses me anew with the wisdom of his equation.

Many persons, perhaps even most, feel that if a girl has a sense of humor, she had better unpack it at the enclosure door. Actually, a sense of humor is vitally important in the cloister. Without it, the enclosure can easily become a spiritual hothouse, where every trifle marks a crisis and pettiness grows into a cult. A sense of humor is like a sweet, clean wind sweeping through our enclosed lives and purifying the small details of them.

The term "sense of humor" has lost much of its fundamental significance in these tortured times of ours, even to the extent that it is often vaguely thought to be something associated with telling jokes and laughing at them. In point of fact, it is a thing rooted in the Divine, for a real sense of humor is what balances the mysteries of joy and sorrow. Without it, we can never hold a true perspective on ourselves or on others. The saints were the true humorists. The better poets were humorists. The ability to see *through* things and to know what is important and what is not, what is to be endured and why we endure it, what is to be tolerated out of compassion and what is to be extirpated out of duty, is dependent upon one's sense of humor. Without the one, we cannot possess the other. A group of dour females with their jaws set grimly for "perfection" and their nerves forever in a jangle would turn a cloister into a psychopathic ward. The joyous, high-spirited girl with a feeling for the splendid sense of things and the delicious nonsense of things is the one most likely to persevere in the enclosure.

When I said good-bye to Father before leaving for the

monastery months later, he gave me a Sacred Heart badge he had worn and this brave counsel: "When you sit on a chair, let the chair hold you." He added, meditatively: "I wish you were thirty pounds heavier . . . but never mind, just don't lose your funny bone." Neurotics? No, not for the enclosure.

Equally preposterous is the idea that the cloister is some sort of female "Foreign Legion". Girls do not enter cloisters to forget the world, but to remember it always in every smallest sacrifice, every prayer, every penance. Least of all do they enter to forget their disappointments in love. Just the thought of a score of lovelorn maidens, locked in an enclosure and sighing their way to sanctity, is so ridiculous that one wonders how anyone could possibly give it a mental nod. The love of God is the strongest driving force on earth. Thousands upon hundreds of thousands have given up their lives simply because they loved Him so much that breath and heartbeat slipped into the inconsequential by comparison. Hundreds upon thousands of young girls have walked into cloisters and never walked out of them because their youth and liberty were the very least to give the One they loved so much.

God's love is not something that catches girls "on the rebound". He is not the second choice of cloistered nuns. Anyone who wants visual proof of all this need only come to an investiture ceremony and see a young and radiant girl leave the cloister in satin bridal gown and crisp white veil, and re-enter it, after the Mass, to be garbed in the simple gray habit and knotted cord of a

Poor Clare, to be convinced that hers is a case of *first* love. Love of God alone motivates a girl to remain in the cloister. He is her first love and her last love, and her love for all the world is part of her love for Him.

The case of the selfish and shiftless deserves an even briefer hearing. The contemplative life is a full, joyous, beautiful life, but it is not an easy life. Nothing makes us laugh more quickly than those romantic pictures of some "contemplative" strolling in a garden at sundown or gazing dreamily up at the trees. This is not to say that we do not walk in our lovely garden on Sundays and feast-days (working in it on other days!), or that we never look up at the curtseying trees. It is only that these pictures are always and obviously slanted at those who think the contemplative life consists of leisurely hours in the choir with the soul steeped in sweetness, followed by a stroll in the garden, and perhaps a spot of embroidery—just to keep fit.

The truth is, the Poor Clare not glad to make her tired way to the dormitory after evening Compline is the Poor Clare not yet born. Her day begins before 2 A.M., and its chants and prayers are punctuated with gardening, sewing, sweeping and scrubbing, washing and ironing, singing and study, typing and painting—among other things. It simply is not a nest for the shiftless. "Brother Fly" was St. Francis' colorful tag for a friar who did not bear his burden of the community's labor and its prayer. "Sister Fly" will find no screen for dozing in the cloisters of St. Clare.

And then: the social misfit. This is perhaps the concept of the contemplative most commonly held by those who do not understand anything about the cloistered life. A girl not fit for the world is certainly not fit for the cloister. The girl who goes to the enclosure to "get away from it all" will most likely be shown to the exit very shortly. There is no room in cloisters for souls of less than universal capacities. It is not girls who looked sourly on the world who make the true contemplatives, but those who might have cried out with the poet: "O world, I cannot hold you close enough!"

What is the point of offering God the "sacrifice" of what we ourselves despise? St. Clare did not loathe her satin gowns, her laughing sisters, her castle home. But she loved God so much more that she gave Him all these lesser loves with a full and singing heart. We see her fine sense of drama, her perfect sense of values, when she dresses herself in her very richest apparel, her most sparkling jewels, to go to the mean little chapel of St. Mary of the Angels, to give them all away. It would not be St. Clare to go to God in sackcloth. No, she went like a bride to her Bridegroom. Each year, before her Feast, when we meditate most deeply on her life, I see our holy Mother that night of her entrance into religion, that night when our Order was born, so young, so gifted, so utterly lovely. The young swains in the city, tapping their toes, and each hoping for a glance of favor from her. Favorone, her father, dreaming of a brilliant alliance for his beautiful daughter. And Clare herself, kneeling in that poor little chapel, her satin and jewels making a pool of light around her as St. Francis stands before her in his patched habit and bare feet, waiting to sign her as his daughter. Would anyone call St. Clare a social misfit?

So much for the negative aspects. The positive aspects are still more elusive to most persons' thinking. Granted a girl has the qualities we have called requisite for the enclosure, what is the real point of it all? Why, asks the world, why? If women want to lead consecrated lives, there are hospitals crying for religious nurses, there are thousands of children green for that cultural, intellectual, and spiritual ripening which only a religious teacher can bring to fruition, there are slums waiting for the clean breath of consecrated love, there are heathens abroad and sophisticated pagans at home. St. Francis' Second Order of enclosed nuns was an ornament of medievalism; to many, it seems about as appropriate in the twentieth century as breastplates on motormen or halberds in the hands of policemen. Yet, each year, the dream of St. Francis and St. Clare beats its wings against the hearts of American college girls and stenographers, salesgirls and beauticians, nurses and private secretaries (to mention the past occupations of some nuns in the Roswell monastery); and American girls find the dream livable and lovable.

Most persons in the world are willing to applaud those who serve God in His members. One wonders why they are so perplexed, even so outraged, at those who choose to serve God in Himself. The doctrine of the Mystical Body of Christ has come of age in our generation. Yet it is still often considered deplorable that clear-eyed, warm-hearted girls believe in that doctrine to the extent of placing themselves in cloister bondage for all the world. But where is there a more essentially practical Christian than the girl who rises in the night to pray for those who do not pray, who performs with joy a whole lifetime of penances for those who sin and wish to do no penance, who chooses the obscurity of the first thirty years of the God-Man's life rather than the activity of the final three, who elects to dwell with our Lady in a cloud of silence and at the immediate beck and call of her Lord?

The point is: God remains the Master of the souls He has created. Who of us will dare to object if God wants certain souls entirely for Himself? If he inspires a girl to be a nursing Sister, a teaching Sister, a Sister in charge of an orphanage, we know such a girl is serving God's suffering, God's youth, God's little ones. May no one wait on Him directly? It is a glorious thing to work for God and thus to be His. It is likewise glorious just to be His.

It is only in surrendering all things that we own everything. It is only by leaving the world that we are sufficiently purified to take the whole world to our hearts. The unique vocation of the cloistered contemplative is to be entirely dedicated to the service of mankind because she is utterly given to God. Because her every breath and action are directed, without any intermediary activity as such, to the most Holy Trinity, she should be more perfectly attuned to the vast hum of creation, to the song of its joy and the groan of its anguish.

Thus no one has the real interests of the world more at heart than the genuine contemplative. She is called to be the mother of all the world. Her enclosed, virginal life is fecund with blessings for humanity. If she tries to make the cloister a narrow corridor in which her own spiritual interests constantly march in procession, she will not persevere. Or, if she does remain in the enclosure, she will be a cross to her abbess and a scandal to her Sisters—possibly a scandal to the world. A cloister is necessarily the home of the universe. Reduce its spiritual dimensions and you lose the lines of God's splendid architecture. It is impossible that a person should sacrifice anything to God without regaining it in an elevated state. This is merely another facet of the truth Francis Thompson learned so thoroughly. The contemplative says: "All that I gave to Thee, I did but give, only to find it again in Thine arms."

From outside the wall, perhaps the regulations concerning enclosure do seem overdrawn. We speak at the parlor grille only to our relatives three times a year, or to priests; to others, only for some extraordinary reason, such as Maria Trapp's giving us recorder lessons, or Dr. Natalie White coming to give me a private course in playwriting. We are not usually permitted to see our friends unless they come in the company of our relatives at the latter's regular visits. (The abbess, of course, may see friends and benefactors of the monastery.) No one is ordinarily permitted for any reason to enter the enclosure even for a minute. When someone does lawfully enter, such as the doctor or dentist, plumber or electrician, he or she is accompanied by the portresses, and the rest of the nuns remain out of sight. We partially veil our faces at the grille in the parlor and the church. We build a high wall around the enclosure garden so that we may never be seen from outside. If, for any reason, such as an operation or X rays, we must leave the enclosure, we are obliged to ask for a written permission from the Archbishop; and when out we may not go anywhere save the place mentioned in the permission.

In all of this, we are not actuated by whim, but follow the very strict regulations laid down by the Church for her cloistered nuns. They are strict because the contemplative life aims at the closest possible union with God, and such an aim necessarily makes extraordinary demands of its pursuivants. They are not fantastic, but seasoned with the wisdom of holy Church. Cloistered nuns are God's property and possession in a very special manner, and the laws of enclosure shield the religious from everything detrimental to her interior union with God. She cannot pass all her days in unbroken adoration at His feet, but she is enabled to recall His Divine Presence with ease and to render Him public homage more frequently than others.

Everything in the cloister speaks of God to the soul. The cloistered nun views from a distance set by her holy enclosure the interests of people of the world, assured thus of the correct perspective. This explains, too, why she has their true interests so completely at heart! The vow of enclosure is the climax and completion of the contemplative's sacrifice and gives to it that all-embracing quality which her particular vocation demands.

In my own case, as in the case of so many others, enclosure has given me the fulfillment of what I had thought it must necessarily abort. "I like to dance and I like to sing", I had told the Jesuit priest at the university, and added that I was prepared to surrender such joys for God alone. And at that very moment, God saw my bare feet dancing around the rude manger Sister Dolores was to fashion from odd pieces of discarded lumber, with the help of a tool kit donated by an unsuspecting benefactor. Unsuspecting, because he was so unschooled in the ways of nuns as to suppose that when he asked to be told of "something you really want for yourself, Mother Abbess—some little feminine extravagance you would not otherwise enjoy", he would be solicited for pretty handkerchiefs or perhaps a sheer wool shawl. He must have bought the tool kit and hand drill with mixed emotions!

And there is the manger, filled with sweet-smelling hay from our Petty's larder out in her cow stall. And here am I, each Christmas devising a new ballet for eager postulants and novices who understand that if anyone in the world should dance at Christmas, contemplatives should! Yet I would scarcely have pirouetted and twirled in a classroom. Sing? The Franciscan Order was born with a song, and Franciscans have been singing ever since. Books? Often, when I am working in the library, I ask in my heart: "My very dear Lord, is there nothing at all I can surrender to you?" For He made me the librarian. Just as He had me learn French years ago so that when the Roswell community would accept a novice from a Poor Clare monastery in France into its own novitiate, I would be able to teach her English. "I like to teach, Father", I had told my Jesuit. Perhaps it sounded a bit wistful to our Lord, so He began "planning".

In one way or another, all of us find ourselves fulfilled and not thwarted in the enclosure. The little outward ways I have touched upon are merely symbolic of the tremendous spiritual fulfillment begun in the cloister and perfected in eternity.

In this very fulfillment, the contemplative simultaneously fulfills her obligation to society. And just as the vow of enclosure enlarges the heart of a nun to gather all of suffering, sinning mankind into it, so does it immeasurably increase her tenderness toward her spiritual Sisters. New postulants are very often struck by this, but it is only the living demonstration of the words of our Mother St. Clare: "If a mother love and nurture her daughter according to the flesh, how much the more ought a Sister to love and nurture her Sister according to the Spirit." There is never a spirit of every-man-for-himself in our cloister. Joys and sufferings are multiplied for each one by the number of nuns in the community.

When Sister Monica's parents made the long trip from Canada for her Profession, each nun worried over Mama's weak health on such a long trip and each one beamed when her prayers were answered by a safe and happy journey. Sister Paula's young friend died in childbirth, and hers were not the only tear-filled eyes. As I write this book, it is being read to the other nuns by

Mother Abbess chapter by chapter, at recreation, simply because it is everybody's business. An abbess who is a Mother Abbess knows what should be made the business of all, and she keeps her community always in a warm circle of united interests. When Dr. White came from the University of Notre Dame to teach me the techniques of playwriting, Mother Abbess told the community of her coming, and a hue and cry would invariably be raised at recreation for details of the day's lesson. And I still like to recall the very evident pleasure of all the nuns when the Redemptorist Father to whom I had first confided my desire to be a religious, when I was sixteen, and who had so warmly encouraged and so wisely directed me was permitted to come to my final Profession ceremony and to preach the sermon. Others of my beloved Redemptorists came, too. "Certainly are a lot of C.SS.R.'s around here", the friars teased me after the ceremony, at the parlor grille. But I was still too moved to return the teasing, with the sound of Father Glennon's voice in my ears again, and the vision of Father Forbes and Father Seifert ministering at my bridal Mass unfading in my heart. My Sisters shared these very personal joys of mine, and to the fullest measure. A poor Clare zippered up into her own personal interests is an anomaly.

So, too, although the different monasteries of the Order are completely autonomous, all are bound closely together by genuine affection. At the Feasts of our Holy Mother St. Clare, our Holy Father St. Francis, and the like, a clamor will unfailingly be made at recreation for "the letters"—meaning the messages from all the other monasteries, telling of a postulant's investiture or an old nun's rheumatism, the storms in Santa Barbara or the snakes in Campina Grande.

It has sometimes been said that St. Clare was a missionary at heart and became a cloistered contemplative only because that was the sole kind of religious life for women known in her day. This never fails to make her daughters bristle! If St. Francis had wanted his Second Order to be a missionary Order, he was just the man to have made that a *fait accompli* in no time at all. No one was ever more "original" than the saint who walked at right angles to everything characteristic of his age. What he founded was a Second Order of enclosed, praying nuns, because that is what he wished to found. St. Clare, on her part, did indeed have a missionary heart. That is why she entered the cloister, to be a missionary to all the world. Any daughter of hers who is not a missionary at heart is in danger of hearing hard words from her seraphic Mother when she meets her after death: "Nescio te!"—"I know you not!"

The enclosed life is the most ancient form of religious life for women, and will always be the most modern. Pope Innocent IV, in his Bull that serves as preface to our holy Rule, gives the purpose of enclosure in a phrase as pregnant with meaning as it is rich in grace: "You, beloved daughters . . . have chosen to serve the Lord in most high Poverty enclosed as to your bodies *in order that* your souls being free, you may minister to Him."

4 MY LADY POVERTY

I beseech you all, my ladies, and counsel you always to live in this most holy life and poverty.

—WORDS OF ST. FRANCIS QUOTED IN THE
RULE OF ST. CLARE

St. Francis and St. Clare were typical children of their age in their speech and manner. When St. Francis envisioned poverty as a beautiful bride, he was sublimating the chivalrous drive within his heart and soul into the supernatural strata. And when he spoke of the "most high poverty" he meant to espouse, he kept the knightly tongue which was the heritage of his class and generation and which he never lost. Grace always builds on nature. In the saints of Assisi, it built on poetic natures attuned to the strains of high chivalry.

Yet this most high poverty was much more than a poetic vision. When St. Francis and St. Clare spoke of "my Lady Poverty", they were not merely indulging in a courtly figure of speech. The business world of the thirteenth century called them fools and dreamers with the same superior smile that the business world of the twentieth century turns on them. Yet these practical men of affairs did not fool even themselves for an instant.

There never was a man less of a dreamer in the world's contemptuous sense of that word than St. Francis. Dream he did, the most splendid dream the world had known since the time of Christ; but he did not fold his dream into lavender and push it wistfully into a drawer of his mind. He put his dream and his vision into such practical form that he turned all of society upside down in an incredibly brief time. And society has not yet recovered from the Franciscan jolt it received in the early thirteenth century. Our Lord Himself promised that it never would recover! The Franciscan family has God's word on it that it will endure to the end of time.

The little Assisian "dreamer" did not sigh over the mystic beauty of our Lord's admonitions in the holy Gospel. He simply followed them. St. Paul had said that we have not here a lasting city, and St. Francis did not intend to put up more than a tent in the extensive camping grounds of the earth. When he set about being perfect in the manner outlined by his Lord, St. Francis showed that literal sense which was rooted in his practical soul and proved so painful to would-be followers of the Gospel who, like Chaucer's scribe, loved to "glosen up and doun". St. Clare, too, was to show herself his literal-minded daughter always. After his death, her hard practicality lay like a boulder in the path of those who tried to rush past her to pull down all St. Francis had built up.

When the businessmen smiled condescendingly at St. Francis, they were only trying to hide the chattering of their teeth. When they called him a dreamer, they were secretly and frantically wishing that he was a dreamer in their sense of that word. The little man with the burning dark eyes who went about dragging stones to repair dilapidated churches, who inspired other young roisterers as wealthy and heedless as he himself had been to give away all their goods and follow him in his highly literal way of poverty, who set out to conquer the whole world with love because Christ had said that was the way to do it, was far too practical-minded for the taste of most men.

His Friars Minor were very soon a major force in society; beautiful young duchesses and princesses were crowding into the cloisters of his Second Order along with girls of humbler birth; and he founded a Third Order so as not to empty all the homes of Italy into monasteries! What these hordes of followers received from him was a way of life revolving in poverty and penance around a Divine hub of Love. The knights and scholars, small farmers and clerks who threw all the externals of their accustomed lives over their shoulders to follow St. Francis had a spirituality as cool in its uncompromising logic as the ground which served them for beds. The highbred ladies who elected to go barefoot, eat the coarsest food, and keep prayer vigils in the night were as hard-headedly practical as St. Clare herself.

The irreligious world is usually willing to give a fond pat on the head to men and women whose "dreams" offer no threat to its own comfort and security. It often applauds them warmly, and sometimes even hails them

as prophets. The case of the God-literal saints whose
dreams take such painfully practical forms is another
matter.

Poverty was truly "most high" to St. Francis and St.
Clare. Most high in the spiritual ideal of the Order, it
must also take the highest place in the material side of
the Franciscan life. And if St. Francis' mystical personifi-
cation of poverty was an exquisite bride, its lowest reflection on the material plane is also intended to radiate
beauty. Strangely, however, Franciscan poverty is thought
by many to be a thing compounded of dirt, want, and
ugliness.

Rumors about life in the cloister are as perpetually
rife as they are usually ridiculous. Yet a girl whose heart
is hammering out the minutes of the days before her
entrance into the Order of Poor Clares has no experi-
mental knowledge to use as a sounding-board for these
fantastic tales whispered to her by well-meaning friends.
There is nothing at all in the life of St. Clare, born in a
castle, bred in luxury, and a true aristocrat to her dying
breath in a narrow cell of the monastery of San Damiano, to indicate that she had a predilection for dirt or
squalor. Yet one of the most persistent rumors about
contemplatives is that they "never use soap". I heard it
and swallowed hard. I learned, much later, that my Novice Mistress had received this same information a generation earlier, and fared far worse than I! For, when I
was led to our little cell in the cloister, its tiny washstand
boasted not only a bright, fat-bellied pitcher on top of it
and a large tublike affair under it, but a gleaming five-

cent plastic soap dish with a new bar of 99 and 44/100 percent pure-it-floats. My poor Novice Mistress, on the other hand, had been led, some thirty years earlier, to a similar cell, which boasted no soap, afloat or asink. Her Mistress had simply forgotten to put it there. And the anguished young postulant set her jaw bravely to face a soapless future. Her anguish was of short duration, for the soap was rushed in the next morning; but that dims nothing of her heroism that first night!

St. Francis and St. Clare loved poverty because Christ loved it, favored it, and chose it all during His earthly life. To them, it was a beautiful thing, an avenue to liberty of spirit and freedom of heart. Its material side had meaning because of its spiritual radiance. The bare feet, the hard beds, the plain food, the forgoing of all earthly claims were real; but they were symbolic, too. St. Francis and St. Clare were the last persons in the world not to respect a symbol, or to offer their own souls or their children an ugly symbol of something lovely. Francis fancied himself a troubadour of the great King, a knight of Lady Poverty; and his poet's heart beat always to the cadences of the loftiest chivalry. No more courteous, beauty-loving man than Francis Bernardone ever lived; and his sanctity was built on a nature as princely as any the world has seen. St. Clare was his feminine counterpart in every way, the truest follower he ever had, one who Englebert makes bold to say understood Francis' ideals even better than he did himself.

The poor little monastery of San Damiano was as much a castle as the luxurious mansion of Favorone, where she was born, simply because St. Clare was a queen and breathed gracious gentility wherever she was. Many could pass themselves off as royal, given the ermine; but only the queenly in soul can be royal in patched serge behind a dishpan. St. Clare was one of these. She trailed beauty after her wherever she passed. And only the kind of queen she was could make of the abbatial position what she made of it, being in fact as truly as in theory "the servant of all the Sisters". Typical of the "prerogatives" she claimed as abbess were those of washing the feet of the extern Sisters when they returned home to the monastery and performing for the sick those services others would call most distasteful.

Her letters, her exhortations, her Rule itself breathe the aristocracy to which she belonged even more by spirit than by birth. She grows lyrical whenever she writes or speaks of poverty. Her Rule is strangely unakin to our modern notions of "rules". She does not offer lists of cautions when she speaks of holy poverty, still less any stern regimental measures, but charms us with such words as these: "I beseech and entreat my Sisters that they be always clothed in poor garments, for the love of the most holy and most sweet Child Jesus, wrapped in poor little swaddling clothes and laid in a manger, and of His most holy Mother." She never dealt with most high poverty in prices-per-yard, for she was that kind of noblewoman who believes all others to be of her own stamp. In fact, St. Clare seems never really to speak of poverty so much as to sing of it. "Cling to this poverty which has made you, my dear daughters, heiresses and queens in the heavenly Kingdom." There is never a Friday when I sit in our plain little refectory and hear those familiar words from the lips of the reader that I do not smooth the mended skirt of our habit over my bare feet a bit more gracefully, and straighten my shoulders a little as I eat our bread and jelly, knowing that a queen has certain obligations to herself and her position.

No one who has read any authentic literature about St. Clare can fancy her having any affection for dirt or for ugliness. The Lady Poverty whom she and St. Francis espoused did not have soiled fingernails.

What we love, we always beautify. What we truly love, we desire others to admire. That is why, even in the lowliest aspect of holy poverty, the material, St. Clare and her daughters know how to turn its full sweetness outward. I have lived in only two monasteries of the Order, but the intimate pictures we exchange with the other monasteries all score the same point: the monasteries of St. Clare are houses of a poverty not grim or drab, but bright and charming. We do not paint things black where we could paint them white. We plant flowering tamarisk around our homemade incinerator because there is no reason why emptying the garbage should not be done with beauty and grace. We stitch our flour-sacking night guimpes with a precision and care that others might reserve for silk and satin. If poverty were thrust upon us, anything would perhaps be good enough. But we chose it, we espoused it. And we mean to clothe it in beauty.

The spirit of poverty must pervade the entire monastery, if St. Clare is to know it is hers. And since that spirit is so essentially a joyous and beautiful spirit, it is very important that its external expression be as appealing as we can make it. We do not compromise poverty when we beautify its externals: rather, we fulfill it. The material expression of a Poor Clare's vow of poverty should be to her as the garments of Lady Poverty, and none of us would leave such a lady's train and veil unwashed and frayed at the edges. We are to preach poverty to the world, and it is our sacred duty to let the world see something of how joyous and appealing voluntary poverty can be.

A new foundation is a school where one learns many precious lessons about material poverty. It is all very well to say it is poverty of spirit alone that counts. And it is true that material poverty is only the shell and not the kernel. However, we do butt our theory against the wall of St. Francis and St. Clare if we press these points *too* far. St. Francis could doubtless have been poor in spirit behind his father's bolts of silk. And St. Clare could have practiced perfect detachment from the luxuries of her castle home while continuing to use them. The hard fact is: they didn't. And there is a great deal more to be said on behalf of material poverty and very simple living than we sometimes like to admit.

We found that out in the very real poverty of a new beginning. We discovered that makeshifts make very good shift. The "traveling light" of which I have spoken before taught us lessons of deep peace and singing joy which we hope never to forget. The old farmhouse which Mother Abbess and the Novice Mistress had coaxed and shaken into monastic form keeps the scars of their invasions. Large bedrooms were divided into three separate nuns' cells by the inexpensive and simple expedient of throwing up cellotex "walls" and putting in separate doors so narrow that even a Poor Clare's extremely uncomplicated boudoir furnishings had to be pushed inside before the partition and doors were set in place. Someone donated gallons of light yellow paint. We can testify to the merits of yellow paint on "cardboard" walls! What you get from your efforts is a small room swimming in golden sunlight, and you hum St. Francis' "Canticle of the Sun" when you make up your bed in the morning. Why anyone should suppose, as some do, that the cell of a Poor Clare ought to be painted a cadaverish gray is a mystery beyond my fathoming powers.

Nothing ever takes up residence in our intellect that has not entered through the doors of the senses. The glad sense of freedom we enjoy by simplifying our materialities as far as possible inevitably makes contact with our spirit. The concept of true spiritual poverty is most easily framed from the testimony of eyes that behold its material expression on every side. St. Francis was not dreaming when he told a bookish friar that an exaggerated love for books could very well end in his needing a servant: "Fetch me our breviary!" He was entirely too practical about poverty as about everything else! We need breviaries, and St. Francis and St. Clare knew it.

But he scored a very good point in his ironic little parable.

The keenest mind we know has the dullness of original sin's bequest upon it when there is question of things spiritual. And that is another reason why material poverty is so important. Few of us make one great leap to the heights of intellectual and spiritual poverty. We get rumorous concepts of it by living in a humbly furnished monastery where we lack conveniences and where we daily make the happy discovery of how very easy it is to get along without the things we once thought essential. An uncluttered exterior life has a very telling effect upon our interior. And an uncluttered interior is the *sine qua non* of contemplative prayer.

Sometimes, too, this material poverty has more than an indirect effect upon the spirit of poverty. It can have a very direct one. The mere fact of having to ask permission for practically everything teaches our judgment to pay out its wealth of pride daily and hourly. The dependence on permissions is an exercise of most high poverty quite as much as of obedience, and anyone with a true Poor Clare vocation comes to glory in this dependence. Our Novice Mistress used to tell us that the multitudinous small permissions we are obliged to ask are our soul's swaddling bands, binding our pride so closely and rendering our independent judgment so helpless that we can claim an ineffable kinship with the Child Jesus and be confident of being carried in the arms of His Immaculate Mother, cared for by her as He was. I have never forgotten that.

New postulants almost invariably find this dependence difficult to practice. Most of the girls who enter have come either from a position where they earned their own living and could dispose of their affairs and their income as they wished or from college, where they chose their courses and extra-curricular activities with as free a hand as they chose their friends. They are not expected to do an about-face in three days. No wise superior expects a girl who sold her own car last month to ask permission to wash her handkerchiefs this month without a general feeling of "Oh, for Heaven's sake!" Actually, the whole point of this tight network of permissions is precisely for Heaven's sake. And gradually a postulant comes to take this kind of dependence for granted. One day, all the explanations and counsels of the Novice Mistress, all the spiritual reading, all the instructions suddenly stand up and fall into place, like small stones in a great and beautiful mosaic. What she has then is the first outline of my Lady Poverty. And even her outline is lovely beyond all words.

We come to take this poverty for granted in time, so that we feel a speechless amazement at one who continues to find its practice impossibly difficult. We had a novice once who, instead of finding the submission demanded by a life of poverty more meaningful as time went on and therefore easier to practice, found it increasingly difficult. I remember hearing her say: "I would rather do without a thing than ask for it." I was stupefied. And then I felt a dull ache in my heart, as though someone had placed a stone in the path of its beating, for I felt sure she would not persevere. She did not.

Things like that make the rest of us feel, not superior or wiser or more spiritual-minded, but only very, very humble. A vocation to follow the way of most high poverty is a precious gift which none of us could possibly merit. Without this entirely gratuitous gift of God, we, too, would find the ramifications of a vow of poverty all too irksome. We would want to rip the swaddling bands and strike out on our own! Like the novice, we could make our very material practice of poverty a violation of its spirit, forgoing materialities for the sake of hoarding up the riches of independence.

The only thing I find difficult about asking permission is the fact that I cannot always fasten upon a superior with the alacrity I would wish in order to ask the permission! In other words, I am not, alas, one of those women in whom the proverb says patience is sometimes found. Yet impatience is also a violation of most high poverty. This lady's perfume so thoroughly permeates a Poor Clare's life that any or all of a nun's faults can be traced to a failure to keep faithful tryst with her. That is why St. Clare releases her daughters from the obligation to obey anyone who may be placed over them who is not bound to this most high poverty.

In the time of St. Clare, it was an accepted course for a wealthy papa to clear his family hearth of a shrewish, unmarriageable daughter by spiriting her away to a monastery and setting her up in business as abbess of the place. If necessary, papa would build a monastery for this purpose. When Church benefices were bought and sold like merchandise, the monasteries of women were by no means immune to the simoniacal plague decimating the Church. Hence, just as young boys were made bishops and cardinals, women who had never lived a religious life or taken religious vows were placed, willy-nilly, over communities of long-suffering nuns. It is very singular that the gentle St. Clare disposes of such situations in one neat phrase: "Let them not obey her. . . ." The conclusion of the phrase is even more striking: "unless she first professes the form of our poverty." That leaves no doubt as to where St. Clare put the emphasis in her way of life: on the most high poverty which was also the be-all and end-all of her Father, St. Francis.

Poverty is called the lowest of the vows of religion when they are treated in an ascending scale. For Franciscans, there is surely a mystic sense in which it is the highest. Poverty is virginal. We are just too poor to own our bodies, to exercise over them that proprietorship by which we could lawfully claim the pleasures of the flesh. And poverty is obedient. We are too poor to clutch at any coins of private judgments to be able to count the currency of our own opinions. We accept the commands of others as an alms to our poverty. We vow enclosure, being too poor to travel! And so we are hugely content with the walled-in tract given us in charity by holy Church, and even manage to house the whole universe in it with us by way of love and compassion.

Indeed, the apex, the depth, the core of a Poor Clare's

life is most high poverty. St. Francis and St. Clare named it aptly.

Sometimes we are startled by the sure insight of persons not bound to poverty by vow. Mother Abbess once obtained permission for an osteopath to enter the enclosure to treat one of our young nuns. The doctor was old, she was a most gracious lady, and she was an expert osteopath. She knew the young nun was a musician, and she herself loved music. So, one day, she asked the Sister to sing a sacred song she named. Only the infirmarian was present with her, so the little nun, embarrassed at being the doctor's charity patient and yet unable to comply with her simple request, explained as best she could that we do not dispose of our songs freely, either. She explained that she could not sing without Reverend Mother's permission, hastily adding that the doctor could ask Mother Abbess. The doctor looked first startled, then a little amused, and then something which the young nun could not decipher. She discovered later what the last enigmatic expression had meant. For the doctor never asked Mother Abbess' permission. Instead, she told Reverend Mother that the fact that we must ask permission to give away a song was more beautiful to her than any song could be, and that she would keep the strains of it longer.

Except that her age and marriage were against her, the doctor might have seemed to show signs of a contemplative vocation!

The daily life of a Poor Clare is a daily unfolding of the mystery of most high poverty. A postulant begins by learning such small details as not letting the water run without necessity, leaving no crumbs uneaten at her place in the refectory, and calling all material things not "my" but "our". We once had a postulant who failed to put her proper laundry mark on her garments. "Is this yours?" a novice inquired, holding out a garden cape. "It used to be mine", replied the fervent postulant; "now it's ours. Take it, if you want it." Then she grows into the novice who wears the insignia of my Lady Poverty with wondering love, folding and unfolding her little white cotton veil with a solicitude she never showed for her wide leghorns and fur toques of other years. She becomes the professed nun who reverences everything in creation with the feeling for symbol which her Father St. Francis had, and who daily renews the vow she made to live forever "without property". It is such a telling Franciscan phrase, that "without property".

A Poor Clare does not vow to live in poverty or to observe poverty or to practice poverty, but to live "without property". She is a happy pilgrim moving through the lanes of creation to the Shrine of the most Holy Trinity, and not wishing to slow down her trek with materialities or the still more burdensome luggage of self-will and its accoutrements. She has not even a handbag for packing little attachments. She is simply "without property" of any kind. And when she has lived out her pilgrimage and lies on her deathbed in the vestibule of the Sanctuary of the Triune God, she will want to repeat the words of her Mother St. Clare, who was courteous to her dying breath: "O my God, I thank you for having created me." For life itself was an alms given by God to her poverty.

Each year on the solemnity of St. Francis, October 4, we sing the beautiful and moving *Transitus*, the commemoration of his holy death. The Franciscan friars are on the other side of the altar grille in the chapel, and we are gathered about the organ on the cloister side. The friars sing out the verse: "*Franciscus pauper et humilis, caelum dives ingreditur*"—"Francis, poor and humble, enters rich into Heaven." Then we sing the response: "*Hymnis caelestibus honoratur!*"—"He is honored with celestial songs." It is a thundering little melody, and the organ accompaniment is very beautiful. But I have to play it by heart; I can never see the musical notes. For my eyes are always full of joyous tears.

5 A LIFE OF PENANCE

*The most high Heavenly Father deigned, by His mercy and grace,
to enlighten my heart to do penance after the example and teaching
of our most blessed Father Francis.*

—TESTAMENT OF ST. CLARE

Postulants often bring with them preconceived notions
of penance, which do not stand them in good stead
when they set about living a penitential life. The whole
structure of the spiritual life is built on paradox, and this
foundation is nowhere more evident than in the concept
and practice of penance. The penances which most girls
come to the cloister steeled to bear are not the telling
penances at all. The penances they have freely elected
beforehand to practice are not very penitential for that
precise reason. However, it usually takes quite some time
for a postulant to digest that axiom!

The first postulant whom Mother Abbess thought
worthy to put to the vote of the Roswell community for
investiture as a novice had come a long way to enter
here. Some of the nuns wondered why she had come so
far and admired her for making so clean a break with all
her former associations. Kathleen had the kind of blue

Irish eyes which change to gray with the force of grave statements. They were darkly gray when Kathy said simply: "I thought a new foundation would be more like the beginnings of the Order. So I came here." It was a charming statement from a very young girl, but it revealed more than Kathy knew of her predispositions for a cloistered life of penance.

A girl who is willing to be taught the true meaning of real penance and to be directed in its practice is the one most likely to persevere. If Kathy had come, as so many do, with a neat little set of ideas about penitential practices, which she would on no account let anyone upset, she would not have been the first radiant bride whom Mother Abbess dressed in white satin and heirloom lace a year later on the day of her investiture as a novice.

Some persons apparently believe that perfection is a matter of feats and formulae. Arm a girl with a discipline and set her running (barefoot, of course) along a racetrack of prayers with evenly spaced hurdles of fasts and vigils, and she is bound to come panting across the finish line as a Poor Clare saint. Actually, it does not work that way.

First of all, there is an air of mystery about the way holy Mother Church keeps repeating the phrase "a life of penance" on the very day when there is nothing at all around to point up the idea. The day of a postulant's investiture with the gray habit and cord of the Order and the white veil of a novice is a day so brimming with gladness and sweetness, so streaming with everything that is young and lovely and pure, that the word "penance" might seem to some like a harsh discord in it all. Poor Clares, however, find the word in perfect consonance with all this springtime display. And the first words the little postulant-bride utters in reply to the Archbishop's question explain the reason why we think penance highly consonant with joy.

His Excellency asks the girl in the white cloud of bridal finery what she desires. Each time I hear the reply in someone's clear young voice, my own heart utters it again: "Your Excellency, I beg you for the love of God . . . to admit me to the habit of the Second Seraphic Order, that I may do penance, amend my life, and serve God faithfully unto death." I *beg* you that I may do penance! We recognize it as our great privilege that holy Church officially accepts our penitential life and offers it to God in union with the infinite merits of Jesus Christ for her errant and suffering children everywhere. Penance undertaken for Love's sake, for the good of souls, lengthens the arms of holy Mother Church, which reach out yearningly to encompass the universal family of mankind, as any mother longs to clasp her children to her heart.

We are not setting up some penitential system for ourselves, but begging to be admitted into an Order whose penitential structure was formed by two of the Church's greatest saints, Francis and Clare, and approvingly sealed by God's Vicar on earth with special grants and most extraordinary privileges. The first and second Orders of St. Francis, his Friars and his Poor Clares, were called the Orders of Penance. Penance is their characteristic stamp. Holy Church has also called them "seraphic". There is something staggering about that term, so much so that it never fails to take me off-guard when we suffix our own title and plea to the Litany of Loreto: "Queen of the Seraphic Order, pray for us!"

Now to call anything human "seraphic" seems much more than merely extravagant. Yet holy Mother Church, who has never been famous for her wild impetuosity or her impulsive fancies, calls St. Francis and his Franciscan family just that: the seraphic St. Francis, the seraphic Order. The seraphim, whom liturgical art offers to our human eyes as spirits afire with love, their pure ardor leaping like flames at the Throne of the most Holy Trinity, are symbolic of the most ecstatic joy. A gloomy seraph might startle even the Triune God! So, if holy Church thinks it not at all inconsistent to say that a religious Order is at once penitential and seraphic, then penance must be a business all bound up with love and spiritual joy. It is.

A postulant who has spent a year in the cloister preparing for the blessed day of her investiture has learned something of this. She knows that in calling her to one of the older Orders in the Church, an order mellowed by seven hundred years and dropping-ripe with canonized saints and blesseds, God has sounded a rare summons. The vast spiritual riches of St. Francis and St. Clare are her inheritance, and when she comes of age as a novice and is ready to claim her inheritance, she must begin to dress becomingly for such a social position and to learn its penitential protocol. That is why she does not kneel before the Archbishop and declare that she is willing to do penance and ready to wear the poor habit of St. Clare. She begs for these privileges. She is not ashamed but eager to fall on her knees and beg before all those assembled for the privilege of doing penance. That is also why we find the idea of penance in perfect accord with the exuberant setting of an investiture ceremony. For this, the postulant entered the Order and for this solemn beginning she has spent a year of apprenticeship. In one sense, the year of postulancy is the most difficult year of religious life; in another sense it is the easiest.

Postulants are young religious creatures who laugh at everything and often at nothing. They giggle in moments of silent solemnity. They have a rare talent for making much noise in quiet cloisters, but themselves hearing none of it. They wear black uniforms and short, thin, black veils, looking from the back like demure young widows and from the front like anything else but that. They sing Gregorian chant not very well but very loudly, and chant the Divine Office in bright, metallic voices—when they can find the place in the fat breviary whose spray of colored ribbon markers they daily entangle in the most intricate knots and loops. They will unfailingly come up with some new variation of the seven-hundred-year-old monastic customs of the house, and are wholly unpredictable. Despite all these things— or, rather, just because of them—they are the objects of the community's very tender and indulgent affection. They are supposed to be the reasons a Novice Mistress grows old quickly. Actually, they are the reasons that she is always young in heart!

Leaving a twentieth-century world to enter a thirteenth-century Order requires a wholesale readjustment, and a wise Novice Mistress knows it. She makes haste slowly, never trying to convert a raw young postulant into a finished model of monastic observance in ten easy lessons. There is really only one lesson in monastic life, the lesson of love. Each day, the postulant with a true vocation masters more of its content. If she is intelligent and basically humble, she will appreciate the corrections given her and accept them with love. If she is too stupid and incurably proud to realize that only good material is considered worthy of perfecting, she will not be kept in the cloister anyway.

Some pious books of the "old school" of spirituality (by which I mean warmed-over Jansenism, not ancient monasticism) seem to teach that the way to make a roaring success of your religious life is to become a real glutton for everything your nature abhors and to eschew anything joyous or agreeable like the plague. Superiors, of course, according to such authors, have a sacred duty to make life as unpleasant for their subjects as they possibly can. If they know that Sister Gandulpha is frightened half to death of heavy machinery, then she is the one to put in charge of the laundry. If postulant Marybelle loves music with all her heart and holds a Master's degree in piano, then she must be kept half a mile from the organ. Novice Libera-nos, who likes nothing better than gardening and has the frame of the athlete she was in the world, should paint illuminations; while Sister Memento-mori, whose delicate fingers make magic with watercolor, should never be allowed to paint.

Such things sound ridiculous, but something of these old notions infiltrates many a modern girl's mind and makes her pause more than once to reflect before applying to enter the cloister. St. Francis was the last man in the world to want to take human nature by the throat and strangle it. If he once instructed a novice to plant cabbages upside down, it was a passing test of his obedience and nothing else. If he sent proud and shy Brother Rufino off to preach in his under-tunic, he also wept tears of remorse and went chasing after him in his own under-tunic, patient Brother Leo bringing up the rear with both habits, to be returned to their wearers as required!

The letters I received from Mother Abbess and my future Novice Mistress before entering were as far removed from anything harsh as letters could possibly be. Yet, for some strange reason which I myself can still not explain, I took it for granted that everything I liked to do and everything for which my nature and education had fitted me was precisely what I would not be permitted to do in the cloister.

I remember presenting God with a quaint little gift as the train carried me to the Chicago monastery. I offered God all the poems I would never be permitted to write. I am sure that He accepted the gift, and that it lost nothing of the qualities I meant it to have when Mother Abbess came into the novitiate after I had been there a few months and said: "You've written poetry, haven't you? Could you write something for the golden jubilee of the monastery next June?" When I wrote it and gave it over to Mother Abbess and the Novice Mistress, they seemed satisfied. And Mother turned back at the door and smiled: "I want you to go on writing poetry. It gives us joy."

On the other hand, of course, the cloister is not a placement bureau. A girl who enters the Order to write or to paint or to develop any other real or supposed talent is making a gross and pathetic error. Ordinarily, superiors are willing and glad to make use of any special gifts a new subject has been given by God, but a girl with a true vocation enters the Order to be a contemplative, not a poet, or a painter, or a gardener. After all, the very highest use of a thing is the sacrifice of it, and a postulant should be prepared to make this *highest* use of everything God has given her. When I mistakenly thought I would not be permitted to write poetry, I made a much happier mistake than the girl who enters to indulge an avocation.

That strange and poignant little offering I made the Almighty of the nonexistent poems, however, was characteristic of a whole set of notions I had somewhere and somehow subconsciously collected. I realize now that I must have had a general feeling in my first days in the cloister of a defendant on the witness stand . . . anything I might say could be used against me! And why? I don't know. The Novice Mistress worried over my thinness and quick fatigue. But when she would ask me in the kindest voice in the world if I were overtired, I would all but sprain my tongue with the too-bright reply: "I? Tired? Oh, no." For some inexplicable reason, I felt certain that if I said "Yes", she would send me home, just like that. The truth was, I was experiencing the full aftermath of months of listening to and attempting to reply to (a great mistake, that last!) the arguments of persons convinced I was making a fatal mistake in entering the cloister. Now that I had achieved the feat of getting inside, I was too tense to sleep at night and consequently half-dying with fatigue in the day. A simple explanation to "Dear Mistress" (as the Novice Mistress is addressed by her young subjects) could have remedied all this without delay. Yet, my mind was stubbornly fixed on the notion that a single admission of exhaustion would occasion my dismissal, and I mentally justified my highly uncandid replies with the private reservation that I was not too tired to be a Poor Clare—was I?

This is one example of the small, twisting sufferings of postulants, and one reason why only the most heartless of persons could ever be hard on them. The first month is usually sufficient to lay to rest most of these mental ghosts whose company comes rattling into the cloister in the dark closets of a new postulant's mind. It does not take her very long to finish with this kind of "penance" and to grasp the fact that the abbess is a *Mother* Abbess and that the Novice Mistress is a *Dear* Mistress, that the nuns are all glad to have another little sister and hope and pray she will persevere as a worthy subject. When a postulant comes to realize that everyone around is raising three lovingly prayerful cheers for her, she gets a very warm feeling in the region of the heart and begins developing reciprocal affection for all these nuns who perform so easily all the monastic practices which come about as easily to her as the rhetoric of Sanskrit.

The feeling of awkwardness clings to a postulant, though, and is her peculiar early penance and sorest trial. Even familiar things seem very strange in the cloister. Addressing an auditorium full of people had never troubled me in the world outside, but reading in a monastic refectory to a community of cloistered nuns quite unmanned me. This is a common trial of postulants; and whenever a new postulant, white of face and set of jaw, is piloted to the reader's dais by the Novice Mistress, the memory of my own young woe is reawakened and flows out in rivers of compassion for this newest victim of holocaust.

A postulant listens to other nuns and novices read in the refectory in blissful ignorance of what lies in store for her. She comes to develop a lively if detached interest in the tablet of charges for each coming week, read out sententiously by the Sister Sacristan each Friday evening after collation. "The charges for the coming week are: Hebdomadaria, Sister Mary Catherine; Versicular, Sister Mary Paula; Reader, Sister Mary Teresa; Server, Sister Mary Anne." But then comes the dread evening when Sister Sacristan says: "Reader, Postulant Kathleen". And Kathy's joyous world crashes in ruins about her black-veiled ears.

When I was a postulant, Dear Mistress cautioned me to read loudly and clearly. Some of the older nuns were a little deaf. I was responsible before God that each nun should hear the spiritual reading. I took all this very much to heart. When Mother Abbess tinkled the little bell which signals the reader to ask the blessing from the hebdomadaria, I yelled, *"Jude, domine, benedicere!"*— "Pray, Lord, a blessing!"—in a voice that rattled the glass panes in the refectory windows and caused each nun to bound six inches off her chair. Dear Mistress had said to read slowly and distinctly. I began the Martyrology for the next day in measured and ponderous tones, brooding over each martyr having his tongue plucked out by order of Emperor Diocletian and deliberating maddeningly over some hermit who was "famous for abstinence". Incidentally, that eulogium always enchants me. As we never eat meat, I figure this is my one chance to become famous in a martyrological sense.

When I had read the praise of the last martyr, a holy lector who sang "alleluia" as the persecutor's arrow pierced his throat, I turned to the appointed ascetical book feeling cold with envy of his happy lot. Nothing would have suited me better at the moment than for one of those silent nuns with head bowed over her bread and tea to stand up and sail an arrow straight through my dry throat. "Alleluia" would have summed up my reactions very neatly. But no one obliged me, and so I shouted my way through a book on the Mystical Body by someone named Jürgensmeier, feeling a dew of perspiration gathering on my forehead and in the palms of my hands.

Finally, Mother Abbess rang the bell for the end of collation, after the lapse of what I calculated to be four or five hours, although the refectory clock placed it at twenty-five minutes. I put down the book, fell on my knees in the middle of the refectory, as is the custom of the reader, to acknowledge her faults in reading, and stumbled down to the postulants' bench to eat our bread and butter with the good appetite of one who has labored hard and long.

I wondered later why I had felt as I did. So does each new postulant-reader in turn. No one has ever analyzed it, but all suffer it.

Last evening when Postulant Joan, who has intelligent dark-brown eyes and is normally graceful and poised, went slinking up to the dais for the first time and asked the hebdomadaria for the blessing in a thin, trembling little voice, I thought of what an especially tender love the Lord must have for His small lectors in monasteries. The wobbly little voice began a continuous process of acceleration, like a snowball rolling downhill, and we ate our bread and tomatoes in such perfect time with it that, although a few had choking spells, we finished collation seven minutes earlier than usual. While we rose, panting, to form procession, Joan completed the glory of her debut by falling off the dais with a loud crash. No one could say she wasn't eager to get clear of the block which goes by the innocent title of "the reader's desk".

Most postulants find the rule of silence very penitential in the beginning, and their learning the monastic signs which we use to curtail necessary speech usually profits monastic silence little at first, as it merely occasions new ripples of laughter from them. For example, our sign for saying that a thing is finished is so much like the gesture small children make for "shame, shame, double-shame", that all new postulants use it with feverish assiduity.

The sign that enchanted me most when I entered was the sign for "man", often used to indicate the exact location of a doctor or workman in the enclosure so that the nuns avoid meeting him. You make the sign by tracing a circle above your head. I took this to mean a halo and was sure that no nun, but some friar convinced of the universal sanctity of his sex, had devised this sign in ages past. I asked Dear Mistress once why we canonize any male who enters the enclosure with this sign. She looked thoughtful and then said she thought the sign was intended to represent a man's hat! I have always loved her for that.

The great silence, as we call the period between evening Compline and morning Terce, is a time of the most profound silence. All work ceases and the monastery is wrapped in thick folds of quiet. The few words the Novice Mistress says to a postulant on her first day in the monastery regarding this great silence may seem to be assimilated by the newcomer, but experience will show how deeply.

The summer's day when Joan entered was calm and sunlit, but we had been in the dormitory for only an hour that night when a fierce windstorm swept down on us. Cells began to disgorge sleepy novices and professed nuns who raced to close the windows in their various departments of the monastery. Of course, no one said a word. No one but Joan. She strolled out of her cell and, finding no stationary novice with whom to exchange the time of the evening, fastened on Dear Mistress instead. That worthy was peering out of her own cell to observe the protective anti-storm measures being taken by her flying novices. "Quite a wind, isn't it?" remarked Joan sociably in a clear, pleasant, most resonant voice. Looking at Joan in the new and shapeless black kimono over the austere white cotton nightgown, with her curling bangs fringing the thirteenth-century little white nightcap, the Mistress could only do what she knew the Lord did: smile.

Almost imperceptibly, while a postulant is taking the first hurdles of monastic life, she is also learning something of the true meaning of penance: what it is and what it is not. Father Philotheus Boehner, O.F.M., had an excellent series of articles on the Franciscan concept of penance in the early 1955 numbers of the Franciscan spiritual review *The Cord*. He clarified the point which remains muggy even to many religious, that penance is essentially a *metanoia*, reversal of direction, and not some kind of spiritual Spartan regimen.

Penitential practices are only peripheral to penance itself. They purify us, they are important in straightening the warped wood of our interior, and they are graciously accepted by God in reparation for our and others' sins if we perform them in love with a truly spiritual intention. If undertaken with disorderly intentions, they can warp our souls more expertly than any number of faults or even sins can.

If a Poor Clare rests in the penitential practices of her monastic life, she is setting herself down on quicksands. If she is pleased with herself over her penitential "accomplishments", she is a stranger to St. Francis and St. Clare. Suspect above all is the desire to perform extraordinary penances beyond those practiced by the community. Thus, the abbess never encourages penitential feats in the cloister. It can happen that God selects a soul to perform extraordinary acts of penance and, therefore, gives her the extraordinary graces and strength necessary for them. But it is not at all the ordinary course of affairs, and even such a soul remains subject to the judgment of her abbess. If the abbess says: No! and the nun insists: Yes! then we can be very sure that the spirit of God is not in the affair.

Nothing so flatters spiritual pride as to indulge in extraordinary penances. The story is told of the monk who fasted continually on a bit of bread and a little water, to the great admiration of his weaker companions, who ate the common fare. This giant of crumbs and droplets later asked to live as a hermit, for his soul required a rarer solitude than he could find in the monastery. He got permission, went to his hermitage—and fainted dead away from hunger the first day! When he returned to the monastery, chastened and perhaps even a bit humbled after several more faints, he asked a very old monk how to explain all this. The old sage smiled. "Son, here the admiration of the other monks was food and drink enough to sustain you well. Alone, you starved."

The common penances of a cloistered community are quite sufficient to aid a soul's sanctification. And the fact that every other nun is doing the same thing you are quite robs such practices of any specious glamour! Getting up in the night to chant the Divine Office and pray for dying sinners is very beautiful. It is also decidedly difficult. "Brother Ass" never quite gets accustomed to being harnessed in the middle of the night. Neither, however, is night rising *too* difficult. No nun ever yet died of it. And the best answer to those who insist that Poor Clares injure their health and shorten their lives by their penances is the hard fact of their longevity. They are notorious for it! Last year Sister Colette, who used to be Postulant Kathleen, wrote some delicious words to the tune "Old Soldiers Never Die." Her version had it that "Poor Clares Seldom Die."

What a postulant finds most penitential about the continual fast is the readjustment. Most girls are accustomed to eating very lightly at mealtime and then dotting the day with cokes and smokes, a hamburger here and a malted there. A cloistered postulant learns that the two slices of bread she gets with her coffee at breakfast mark "finis" of refections until dinner. There are no coffee breaks in a monastic morning. At dinner, she is told to eat more potatoes and vegetables than she probably wants, because this is the only full meal of the day, on the strength of which she must work and pray until the next day. There is also a light evening refection, called "collation", which is quite sufficient for any normal girl.

There is nothing spectacular about the Poor Clare fast, and St. Clare wants it waived in favor of the sick and the delicate. Neither St. Francis nor St. Clare ever tried to hang the Order on a peg of fast and abstinence. It is only one of the penitential means to achieve real penance, the *metanoia*, and is more difficult for some and less difficult for others.

I was delighted when I entered to see how the holy Rule gathers "Brother Ass" up into its spiritual embrace. We dine by the liturgy. On the great penance days, we take our dinner from the floor. We sit back on our heels and eat boiled potatoes and turnips, and think lovingly of our Father St. Francis, who sat just like this in a thirteenth-century refectory. On ordinary days, we sit on our chairs behind the plain tables; and we can determine the rite of the Office of the day just as easily from what we see in our dinner plates as from what we read in the directory. Mashed potatoes indicate a solemnity!

I was impressed, because I thought all this so truly and deeply spiritual. *Everything* in a Poor Clare monastery is regulated by the liturgy, even the way the potatoes are cooked. It is one more evidence of how thoroughly St. Francis and St. Clare immersed themselves and their Rule in the life stream of holy Church.

All these things at which many in the world are aghast: the fasts, the abstinence, the hard beds, the night vigils, the bare feet, are not what constitute the inner *metanoia*, not the great penance of the contemplative nun's life, which is simply putting off the old man and putting on the new. She is helped in this by the varying characters and temperaments of those whose lives are so very closely interwoven with hers in the cloister. There are no transfers for cloistered nuns, no new appointments. I remember Mother Abbess telling us when we were novices: "Always keep your love for one another tender and real, because with us it is a matter of 'Until death do us part!' "

The Poor Clare is helped to practice penance, too, by the fact that cloisters provide no spiritual closets for the skeletons in her own soul. The enclosed life has a fundamental sweep about it. You simply have to call a spade a spade, and your faults—faults. An enclosed nun cannot camouflage her lack of true being by a great flurry of doing. She cannot "lose herself" in her students or her patients or her orphans. She has to find herself all day long, and she does this by finding God. The first is her penance, the second is her joy. Together, they are her *metanoia*. The pain of discovering herself and the bliss of discovering God are what let her discover all the world and make her understand that the universe is her personal, God-given charge. Patience, fraternal charity, meekness, humility, and all their brave company then stand up and take on entirely new form.

Such notions of penance have begun to form in the soul of the young postulant-bride who kneels to ask the Archbishop please to permit her to do penance as a Poor Clare. She begs to be admitted to St. Francis' Second Order of Penance. And the organ peals for her, and the altar is massed with flowers for her, and everything in the monastery rejoices with its youngest penitent, because when St. Francis wrote his first Rule for his Order of Penance, he set down these words: "And let them take heed not to appear sad exteriorly like gloomy hypocrites, but let them prove to be joyful in the Lord, and merry and becomingly courteous."

6 THE DIVINE OFFICE, WORK OF GOD

The Sisters shall recite the Divine Office after the custom of the Friars Minor; wherefore, they may have breviaries.

—RULE OF ST. CLARE

A monastic investiture ceremony, when a young girl is formally engaged to a Lover Who is the most beautiful of the sons of man, contains the essence of romance. I had seen investiture ceremonies elsewhere before I entered, but I was quite unprepared for the way the Poor Clares do it. I am still always completely unprepared!

The three little black-garbed figures dotting the rows of gray habits in the Roswell monastery had become dear and familiar figures. Kathleen laughed as merrily, startled us as often, and broke as many jars as did her two postulant companions. But now it was Kathy's investiture day, and when the community gathered at the foot of the dormitory stairs that morning, it was no familiar black-skirted figure whom Mother Abbess led down to us, but a princess.

Kathy wore palest ivory satin and lace. She looked like a debutante, and was one in the very truest sense of the word. Her long satin train was looped up over her arm, waiting to trail its full glory in the chapel. The dark curls were not flattened back today, but fell loose and shining about her face under the cloud of veil with its creamy lace panels. Kathy had a corsage of white roses against her shoulder and a string of pearls about her neck. The Irish eyes were not pools of blue laughter this morning; they were dark and dreaming. We all caught our breath, as we always do—all a little shy of this lovely young bride and most of us seeing her through a faint mist of the tears a great tenderness always evokes.

Mother Abbess herself had made Kathy's dress and veil, and I am sure that St. Clare hovered over the stitching and supervised all the fittings. For no one felt more strongly on the point of garbing Christ's brides in the finest than did St. Clare. She had worn the most gorgeous of her rich gowns on the night of her own investiture by St. Francis, and she had bedecked herself with jewels. And to this day, we cherish her sense of symbolism and drama. Since Kathy's investiture, five brides in the world have donated their beautiful wedding gowns to the monastery, in the hope of having them worn by a bride of Christ. It is an exquisite gesture, and surely the Divine Bridegroom will bless the married lives of girls so generous and spiritual-minded.

Layfolk are not slow to grasp and love the symbolism of an investiture. People are always spotting the wrong lady for the mother of the bride, because so many ladies are weeping! After one of our investiture ceremonies, a number of the community's friends selected the lady

who was weeping most copiously of all and began con-
gratulating her: Her daughter was such a lovely girl, she
must be so proud, etc., etc. The lady was astonished.
"But she is not my daughter! I just drove my friends to
the chapel for the ceremony. I am not a Catholic. I never
saw the monastery before."

The postulant-bride leaves the enclosure for the Solemn High Mass. In the ordinary course of events, it is
the last time she will ever go out of the cloister. And
when the young bride kneels all alone on the satin-
covered prie-dieu in the sanctuary, because this Bridegroom is visible only to the attending angels, it would
require a heart totally devoid of poetry and quite dead to
romance not to be touched and quickened.

Less touching but just as colorful have been the
postulant's material preparations for this great day. It is
surprising how quickly one loses the knack of walking
lightly and gracefully on high heels. Poor Clare postulants wear soft-soled bedroom slippers all the time, for
the clomp-clomp of shoes would be entirely anachronis-
tic in a cloister of barefoot nuns. Just before my investiture, Dear Mistress asked me if I would be comfortable
in a pair of very high-heeled white sandals given by
another novice's sister. I blithely assured her that I would.
Being of a practical turn of mind, the Mistress reminded
me that our bridal dress had a long train; I had better
practice. Practice I did, clicking up and down the novitiate dormitory hall in the high-heeled white sandals
over black cotton stockings, with our postulant black
skirt trailing an inglorious train made of bath towels

safety-pinned together. I genuflected, turned, and flung the bath towels about with what I considered was quite some grace of motion, even if a year of bedroom slippers had left me a bit unsteady on the high heels.

Such homely memories, though, are quite lost in the glory of investiture morning, and the bride is caught up into a world of utter beauty, where her Lord and Lover dwells. The mystery of the Mass enfolds her and sets her on the threshold of this new beginning.

After the Mass, the significant little heap of garments is blessed by the celebrant: the gray habit, the cord, the white veil. Then the Archbishop gives the bride a lighted candle wound around with flowers and trailing ribbons, over which some novice has labored and perspired in the early hours of this morning. Holding the lovely torch, the bride leads the procession of clergy, religious, family, and friends back to the great double doors of the enclosure where the nuns are awaiting her, each holding her own lighted candle. The people glimpse the mantled and veiled figures and look at the inviting candles, though they cannot see the joyous faces of the nuns who sing out the Church's invitation to Kathy: "Come, spouse of Christ, receive the crown which the Lord has prepared for thee forever." And the wonderful psalm "*Laetatus sum*"—"I rejoiced at the things that were said to me; we shall go into the house of the Lord!" Kathy kneels for a solemn blessing from the Archbishop, rises to sweep a last good-bye to everything outside the cloister, and then she is caught up into the procession of nuns who conduct her to the cloister choir singing: "One thing I have asked of the Lord, that I may dwell in the house of the Lord all the days of my life."

At the open grate in the cloister, Kathy is divested of her satin and lace and pearls. Mother Abbess drops the gray habit over her head and girds her with the white cord while the Archbishop recites some profoundly beautiful prayers, all of them shot through with that telling phrase: ". . . a life of penance". Kathy slips out of the high-heeled white sandals. She kneels and bows her head over the little wicker basket held by the Novice Mistress, and soon the basket is full of the shining holocaust of Kathy's curls, which will later be boxed and ribboned by some novice and given to Kathy's mother. The small shorn lamb kneels at the grate with a little white cap over her cropped hair, and Mother Abbess fastens the white guimpe and pins the white veil. She places a wreath of flowers around the white-veiled head, and the same angels who sang at St. Clare's investiture take up the song they sang at St. Mary of the Angels in 1212.

The wonderful ceremony is over, except for one thing, Kathy's new name. The nuns always maintain that this placement is an act of supreme cruelty to the community. Speculation on the postulant's religious name has been the burning topic at recreation for weeks past. Mother Abbess has been teased and tempted and cajoled, all to no avail. Only when the powers of the community's endurance are strained to their utmost, with every nun leaning out of her stall at a dangerous angle for fear she might not hear the Archbishop say it, does His Excellency finally say: "My daughter, in the future you shall no longer be called Kathleen, but Sister Mary Colette of Jesus." You can always hear the nuns exhale after that.

Sister Colette sets down the holy Rule, the crucifix, and the breviary that have been placed in her hands, and while she embraces Mother Abbess, the schola intones the jubilant psalm *Conserva me*. The Novice Mistress takes Sister Colette from one nun to another to receive the embrace of each and her whispered words: "May the Lord grant you peace and perseverance." And the singers continue the psalm: "Preserve me, O Lord, for I have put my trust in Thee. . . . I will bless the Lord, Who hath given me understanding. . . . I set the Lord always in my sight. . . . Thou hast shown me the ways of life, . . . at Thy right hand are delights. . . ."

The psalms which hold an investiture ceremony in a kind of liturgical embrace are part of what forms the great work of a Poor Clare's life: the Divine Office, called by the founders of monasticism the *opus Dei*. The canonical hours form a glorious moving circlet around a center of the Mass; and even new postulants who are entirely bewildered by the pattern of the Divine Office are caught up in some fashion into this great, solemn movement. There is nothing in the life of a Poor Clare which is not regulated, colored, and elevated by the Divine Office. I have said that the rite of the day's Office determines what we find in our dinner plates. It also determines how we dress, the kind of work we do, how much we recreate, and it creates an atmosphere of joy or reflective sorrow or eager anticipation throughout the whole monastic building as well as in each nun's soul.

If the Office is an ordinary "double" or a common "simplex", we eat the commonest food we have, do our ordinary work in our work habits, and have one hour of recreation in the evening. On penance days, the recreation is omitted. But when the Office is of the "first class" rite, the nuns blossom out in Sunday veils and "good" habits, doing what we call our "white collar work"—painting, crocheting, learning polyphonic music, and the like. These are the days when I write down the poems I have housed in my heart during hours of work. There is usually an extra hour of recreation on such days, and no one is obliged to work at darning, mending, and patching during the recreation; she may do small-scale white collar work instead. Best of all, she has much extra time to spend in the choir.

This business of dressing according to the greater Feasts is considered so important that one must have a very authentic excuse and a "*cum permissu superiorum*" to turn up at a first-class Vespers in a work habit. When we were building the new chapel and choir, first Vespers of St. John the Baptist surprised us all balanced precariously on ladders, painting at a great rate, perspiring in the thick June afternoon, and our cheeks and noses speckled with white paint. Even in such straits, we had to get permission from headquarters to go to Vespers in our "fatigue suits" and not climb into our dubious finery for St. John. Consulted, Mother Abbess (who is a direct descendant of King Solomon on her mother's side) pronounced that it would be all right this time because, after all, St. John the Baptist was not the man to be fussy about changing his camel's-hair shirt. Even for this indulgence, Reverend Mother had a highly liturgical reason!

All that may sound unimportant, but actually it is not. People in the world dress for occasions. We wear our poor best for the liturgical solemnities because those are the great days of our lives. It is part of the Franciscan spirit. A true Poor Clare has a very deep respect for occasions, and to elevate all the material aspects of her life to the spiritual plane is a sign not of a childish whim but of a profound and highly practical spirituality.

A rough habit and a cord just about summed up what St. Francis considered the necessities of life for his sons. St. Clare needed little more for her daughters. Yet, to their extraordinarily brief list of essentials, both were quick to add a breviary. Books were rare and expensive in the thirteenth century and few women could read. Even highbred ladies of wealth and position were often illiterate. But St. Clare devotes a chapter of our Rule to the Divine Office and wishes each of her Poor Ladies to have a breviary, cost what it may. "They shall recite the Divine Office after the custom of the Friars Minor; wherefore, they may have breviaries."

When St. Francis was lifted to the heights of ecstatic prayer on Monte La Verna, he never forgot the canonical hours. In fact, his spiritual elevation sprang from them, being drawn by the love and grace of God from the liturgy Francis loved. His stigmatization occurred around the Feast of the Exaltation of the Holy Cross, showing that the Lord Jesus, Who appeared to St. Francis as a crucified seraph, had Himself a very nice liturgical sense. The stigmatization would have been ill-placed during Christmastide.

In his lonely solitude, St. Francis permitted Brother Leo to come to him at night to recite the Office with him. When Francis overslept, the falcon who abode with him in his little hermitage would perch on the saint's shoulder and squawk in his ear until he awakened Francis. Incidentally, Sister Sacristan in Roswell never hears this tale without getting a thoughtful look in her eyes. It is her duty to awaken the community each night-time for Matins and each dawn for Lauds, and an oblig-ing falcon could aid her mightily in her efforts to rouse some of our more talented sleepers.

The Divine Office never fails to overwhelm a new postulant with its intricacies. A postulant stands next to the Mistress in choir for the first few weeks, and begins to suspect herself of being a moron. For, just when she is certain she has struck the correct position, the Mistress is sure to swing her clockwise by the elbow. If she thinks it is time to stand, all the other nuns unfailingly fall on their knees, and she feels the familiar hand pulling her downward. If she chants: "Amen", all the others sing out: "Deo gratias!" When the two versiculars proceed to the middle of the choir, she invariably trots after them, to the great amusement of the novices, who have for-gotten they did the same thing last year. But to the blushing postulant, there is nothing humorous in all this, because she does not suspect that each postulant before her has been just as awkward and just as thoroughly bewildered.

After I had once made some particularly idiotic mistake, I tried to gather together the shreds of my postulant dignity by telling Dear Mistress that that part of the Office was not printed in *our* breviary. She looked very long-suffering, but only sighed in a tired voice: "Child!" Personally, I still think I was unjustly handicapped by being in the group with a postulant who was a *rara avis* in this line. Mabel always said "Amen" at the proper time. She did not chant like a broken-down factory whistle (my style), but like the professed nuns. The ribbon markers in Mabel's breviary always seemed to leap out of the proper page at the proper moment as needed. Mabel knelt, rose, and turned to the altar in a manner that left the Mistress little to do and much to admire. There just never was another postulant like Mabel, and I will not be the one to say that she did not persevere on that account. But, anyway, she did not.

After about two months, the mysterious rubrics of the Divine Office suddenly begin to make some sense to the postulant. And what she had already come to reverence with a vague, half-understanding love now commences to shape her life and to transfigure it. She discovers how perfectly the Office expresses her joys and her sorrows. Then she discovers that the Office is her joy and her sorrow, the joy and sorrow of the universe and all men in it. She lets herself be carried in the arms of its joyful feasts, and her soul mourns with its sorrowful mysteries.

I thought I loved the changing seasons of holy Church in the world, but what Maurice Zundel so aptly called the splendor of the liturgy had been hidden from me under a heavy veil. Now, the breviary drew off that veil, and I discovered the meaning of my own life, my vocation, my destiny, and the destiny of all men in what I beheld.

In Advent, we gather each Sunday evening in the community room under the big green wreath that swings above our heads on long purple ribbons. There are four tall candles set in the wreath, and each week Mother Abbess lights one more, first sprinkling the wreath and us with holy water and then reciting the day's collect, full of the Church's immense yearning for the coming of the little Redeemer. "Come! Come! Come!" And we stand under the wreath where the Isaiah-candle burns, and the St. John Baptist-candle, and the St. Joseph-candle, joined at last by the Mary-candle; and we sing: "*Veni, veni, Emmanuel*". The whole monastery is on tiptoe with expectation, and the colored ropes and bells and stars that happy-faced nuns will soon be draping and pinning all over the monastery take their meaning from these prayers and these Office chants.

The last days of Advent, we stand in our choir stalls and sing the glorious O's of the waiting Church. The youngest postulant, looking terribly important and heavy with her responsibility, goes to the tower to ring the great Maria-bell (Miguel, the smaller bell, will join Maria on Christmas Eve), while the nuns chant: "O Wisdom . . . O Key . . . O King . . . Come!"

I thought I used to be on mental tiptoe with expectant joy on Christmas Eve at home. But in the monastery! The Divine Office seems scarcely able to contain itself on the vigil of Christmas: "Tomorrow . . . tomorrow . . . tomorrow", it whispers over and over again. And at the end of Christmas Matins, just at midnight, when Mother Abbess lifts the familiar small Bambino out of the fluff of blanket next to her choir stall and walks the long avenue of the choir to place Him in the manger Sister Sacristan has built beneath the altar, we sing: "*Te Deum laudamus*"—because what else is there to say?

It is the same with the Church's sorrows. In the monastery, you do not attend Lenten services or assist at the ceremonies of Holy Week. You suffer Lent with the breviary and you are consumed by the Offices of Holy Week. The nun singing one of Jeremiah's lamentations at the lectern gathers the anguish of the ages into her heart. It escapes in her voice. All the nuns singing the recurring "Jerusalem, Jerusalem!" are raising a terrible cry of importunity that the world will let itself be saved.

The Divine Office is so tremendous that it is no wonder the new novice feels her knees buckle when she is first appointed to officiate. Postulants join in the chants of the Office, but only after investiture as novices may they serve as versiculars or chant a lesson at Matins, and experience the alien sound of their own thin voices singing out alone in the big choir. I received the holy habit on June 26, and I was jubilant when told that I would chant my first lesson at Matins on June 29, Feast of Ss. Peter and Paul. But when I found myself at the lectern with no one else saying anything at all, my bones turned to water and my teeth began an intricate little tap dance that made my voice sound very odd even to my-self. There I stood, with the whole universal Church waiting to use my voice. I had a sudden intuition of the size and significance of holy Church and the size and significance of Sister Mary Francis. The intuition over-whelmed me. The lesson was from the Acts of the Apostles and began: "Peter and John went up to the temple." I was sure I would never get them there.

The Novice Mistress always stands beside a novice at the lectern, supposedly to correct her mistakes. My guess is, it is also that she is handy to give first-aid as needed. But it is a very wonderful thing to feel yourself dwarfed by the magnificence of the Divine Office. It is the best way to reckon your true and only glory, that of being lost in the glory of God.

The circling feasts trace the same orbit every year, but they are always new. Someone has beautifully expressed this by saying that our souls are climbing up the moun-tain of God, and each new year we have a different perspective, from a new height, on the mysteries, which themselves remain the same. The very words of the Divine Office overflow the canonical hours into all the exercises of our life. We begin our work and our recre-ation with the Church's summons to her Sanctifier: "*Veni, Creator Spiritus!*"—"Come, Creator Spirit!" When we assemble at Chapter to await Mother Abbess' corrections and admonitions, the breviary lends us an appropriate psalm for the occasion: "As the eyes of the handmaids are on the hands of their mistress. . . ." When a postulant has received the vote of the community for her investiture, all the postulants and novices troop into the Chapter and raise a jubilant cry from the breviary: "*Laudate, pueri!*"—"Praise the Lord, ye children!" So it goes.

The Divine Office is our soul's atmosphere and it even creates our weather. The skies may send down sheets of rain on the Feast of our holy Mother St. Clare in August, but no one cares or even seems to notice, because the Divine Office declares that "Now the shining brightness of Clare has filled the whole earth."

Our Father St. Francis was very particular about the rubrics of the Divine Office. No passage in the breviary may be chanted haphazardly, no psalm left unfinished. He was reciting the psalm "*Voce mea*"—"With my voice I have cried to the Lord . . . lead my soul out of prison"—when Sister Death bent down to kiss his lips. He finished the psalm. And then he received her kiss.

7 OBEDIENT VIRGINS

I, together with a few Sisters whom the Lord had given me a little time after my own conversion, willingly promised Him obedience.

—TESTAMENT OF ST. CLARE

The ceremonial for profession of vows in the monastery is so preoccupied with the vow of virginity that you would think it the only vow the novice was making. In ancient times, the ritual was known simply as that for the "consecration of virgins", and it is a great mistake to think that the state of virginity solemnly vowed to God is no different from the state of single persons in the world. The unmarried woman is free to change her state of life whenever she wishes. The consecrated virgin has given her entire future into the hands of God, signed with a changeless seal. The motives of a girl in the world for remaining single may be as varied as the sands on the seashore. The motive of the religious is unique: she wishes to give herself, body and soul, to God.

The positive aspect of holy virginity is far too often entirely ignored. Virginity is thought to be a mere abstention. Many, dazzled by the coruscating if specious logic of psychologists of the Freudian school, think it a blight on the development of the personality. One cannot experience the fullness of happiness in the virginal state, they maintain. It needs only one long look at the faces of nuns, one long listen to their laughter, to blow this proposition sky-high—or, better, earth-low.

Even some religious persons never enlarge their concept of virginity beyond the idea of a forgoing of carnal pleasures. Yet this is only the low gateway to the marvelously beautiful concept of virginity as a positive thing. When a young Poor Clare has completed her canonical year as a white-veiled novice, she kneels in the choir on her Profession morning, and the schola sings her a message from God. What she hears is an exquisite lyric responsory whose words say nothing at all of forgoing or abstention or sacrifice. "Come, my chosen one . . . the King has greatly desired your beauty!" Any good woman is flattered by the love of a good man. What stirs in the heart of a girl who has the word of holy Church on it that the great King of creation has selected her and greatly desired her loveliness for Himself! The choir goes on singing, and the novice hears the wonderful words repeated, this time as the explanation of why leaving everything else in the world is no great thing in the face of being so chosen. "Forget your people and your father's house . . . for the King has greatly desired your beauty."

When the novice has pronounced her vows and the black veil is placed on her head, the first words the Church puts into her mouth are gloriously significant. They are the words of a girl more loved than Juliet ever was. And she cannot say them, she must sing them: "Christ has set a mark upon my face, that I should admit no other lover but Him." There is no mere negation here! Here is the surest and profoundest love in the world. And when the wreath of white flowers is pinned on the black veil, the newly professed nun breaks into song again. Does not every new bride sing? In this case, we hear how completely the young religious has passed into the kingdom of the spirit. For she stands at the open grate in her poor gray habit and common black veil, and she sings: "The Lord has clothed me with a gilt-embroidered robe, and He has adorned me with inestimable jewels." No more is this the language of negation. This is surely the most positive of statements.

Virginity is not only a giving, but a receiving. If properly understood, it is a glorious enrichment. A woman who knows herself to be completely cherished is a woman of confidence and poise. This carries over into the spiritual life and gives a Poor Clare interior confidence and spiritual poise in whatever sorrows and trials may lie ahead. She does penance, she may suffer in multitudinous and soul-searching ways. But she knows she is loved, cherished, chosen. That is really all a woman needs.

Consecrated virginity is not sterile, but fecund with spiritual life. The psalms the contemplative loves write her history in words of flaming truth: "Many are the children of the barren, more than of her that hath a husband." Many as the number of souls in the world are the children of a cloistered nun. The life of souls stirs always beneath her heart, and a sinner reclaimed leaps for joy in the warmth of her soul, for it houses him. A Poor Clare vocation is a vocation to be the mother of the world. It is a reflection of the vocation of the Mother of God, whose glorious exaltation is unthinkable without virginity. It is likewise the fullest participation for a woman in the life of holy Church, the Bride of Christ; and the strength of the Church increases with the sacrificial life of each of her consecrated virgins. Virginity is the essence of the religious consecration to God and its most positive aspect.

Obedience, on the other hand, may be called a disciplinary vow. Yet, religious life without obedience would be a three-ring circus. Complete, continual, unswerving obedience comes naturally to no one. Our first parents planted the seed of disobedience in the soul of each of their children. It is true, though, that the seed bears more luxuriant fruit in some, and only sickly plants, easily uprooted, in others. In other words, obedience comes easier to some characters than to other characters.

A vocation to the cloister does not presuppose an insatiable thirst to be told what to do. Most modern girls are remarkably adept at ordering all details of their own lives. And most girls find obedience the big hurdle in religious life. Self-will is said to die only fifteen minutes before we do—or is it fifteen minutes after! At any rate, the feeling of being captain of this ship, mistress of one's own affairs, is the last luxury nature is willing to forgo.

To add to nature's objections, the devil has a very fine sand especially prepared for the state of emergency into which each new religious vocation throws all hell. He scatters this light powder into a postulant's eyes during the first weeks of her religious life so that she can no longer see certain details of her past. Being told at every turn what to do and how to do it in approved monastic form, she forgets that she has actually been taking orders all her life. We all move within a tight orbit of obedience even in adulthood, obeying superiors ranging from the dean of the college or the head of office personnel to the traffic policemen who tell us when we may cross the street and when we may not.

Now, to turn a jaundiced eye on this matter of obedience is, like Atlas, to "miss the point entirely of the grand Deific theme" (as Sister Madeleva has so charmingly expressed it). To turn on it, instead, a full and loving gaze is to come into immense riches of liberty and the most complete exercise of our freedom. People in the world are forced to obey man-made laws and workaday restrictions. Contemplative nuns freely elect to obey a monastic Rule inspired by God. The girl pounding her typewriter may be pounding for nothing but dollars' sake and wishing she could stop. The Poor Clare sweeping the monastery cloisters is doing it for God's sake and prefers sweeping, at that particular hour, to any other occupation in the world.

Obedience really transfigures our religious life, and that is why the expression of our formula of vows is so telling again in this instance. The novice promises not just to obey orders or to practice obedience but to "live *in* obedience". The phrase has a splendid ring to it, as though she were throwing up imposing castle walls around her entire life. And that is precisely what she does. She makes her whole future existence a kind of vast dwelling place through which she can walk in perfect security always.

An obedient religious simply cannot blunder while she obeys. The superior may be wrong in commanding, but the subject is still right in obeying. It is a wondrous alchemy by which the brass of an imprudent order is unfailingly changed to gold for the one who obeys it. Too many persons think of being bound to obey. Actually, it is the headiest exercise of our liberty to be free to obey. Adam was the lord of the world when he was free to obey. When he surrendered that glorious freedom in order to disobey . . . well, which human heart does not keep the record of his sorry loss?

The idea of the nobility in being free to surrender our wills even in the smallest matters is never, however, swallowed at one gulp in the first weeks of postulancy. The little fetters by which we freely elect to be bound to our dear Lord seem irksome until we get the taste of the world out of our mouths and forget its talk and its false values. When I was striking out into the deeps of the Divine Office as a postulant, Dear Mistress told me to turn to the *Magnificat* at Vespers each day. I did not turn. Next day, she inquired into this curious fact; and I informed her brightly that I knew the *Magnificat* by heart, expecting to be commended for lore so outstanding in one so young. Dear Mistress, however, did not pat me fondly on the shoulder. She did not even smile, proudly or otherwise. She said in a flat, firm voice: "That is entirely beside the point. Turn to the *Magnificat* and read it. It is the custom." That is the first of my store of recollections about obedience in small matters.

One of the nuns who impressed me most when I entered was a certain old warrior who was bent one-third her height over a stout cane. Sister Mechtilde had a way of looking at you that was most disconcerting. She squinted one old eye completely closed and looked with the unblinking other into the depths of your soul. Or so I suspected. She always took the measure of new postulants in this searching manner, and I was not the first or the last to shrivel up into a shocking new sense of my own deficiencies under the beacon of that one eye. Sister Mechtilde's voice was deep and sonorous; and of all her stock phrases, the one that always froze me solid was her resounding "It 'tisn't customary." Her double-t effect added immeasurably to the force of this statement, making it an indictment.

Because she was so ancient and had seemed to grow into the very walls of the monastery with the years, Sister Mechtilde was accepted by all as a kind of unofficial Novice Mistress. Sister Mechtilde always started off to the choir or the refectory in advance of the procession on account of her infirmity and years, thus gaining the vantage point she held on all the bright young things invariably doing the wrong things. A postulant merrily ladling out her own soup at dinner when she came early to the refectory as reader would not ladle merrily for long. "It 'tisn't customary", Sister Mechtilde would boom at the brash young creature. (Postulants are supposed to ask a professed nun to serve them.) A novice with her cord knotted at uneven lengths might escape the eye of the Mistress, but was sure to get an accusing point of the cane from Sister Mechtilde and the famous: "That 'tisn't customary."

One evening, after collation in the refectory, Mother Abbess mentioned the fact of some communities filing up to receive Holy Communion beginning with the youngest instead of the oldest. It seems there was some discussion afoot on the point. With the privilege of many years, Sister Mechtilde squinted up at the head table and boomed aloud: "Well, it 'tisn't customary." I shall never forget the wild thrill we postulants felt! It was not only the delicious excitement of having someone speak in the refectory, but the undreamed-of and highly unorthodox bliss of hearing Mother Abbess herself told that this thing was not customary. We postulants had long since come to the conclusion that anything which seemed expeditious to us 'twas not customary. And suddenly Reverend Mother herself was thrust into our inglorious company! We giggled wickedly and quite deliriously.

Months later, some of old Sister Mechtilde's transparently childlike obedience began to take hold of my admiration. Now I saw the keen intelligence and the deep love in that one eye that scrutinized me so thoroughly. I glimpsed something of the heroic spiritual stature of this ancient nun whose obviously fiery native temperament had been broken in that beautiful sense of the word which we use when we talk of an unruly (and, therefore, useless!) steed being "broken" into the handsome and disciplined creature we admire in the thoroughbred racer. Adam and Eve threw all our spiritual limbs out of joint. Those limbs must be broken if ever they are to be set perfectly, so that we can walk unfalteringly again as children of God and heirs to the Kingdom. Obedience does this like the most skilled of doctors. And only the very stupid or the hopelessly coarse can conceive such a remedial breaking as merely a smashing.

Sister Mechtilde had certainly not been smashed! Even now, several years after her death, my memory envisions her marvelous vibrancy so warmly that she seems as alive as the nuns breathing around me. She had only been beautifully broken by a long life of obedience until her spiritual gait was swinging and completely sure. I think of that bent old frame, and I remember how tall and straight the soul stood because ancient Sister Mechtilde had not just obeyed but had "lived in obedience" all her long life. Obedience had found the marrow of her soul. And she had achieved such glorious freedom to obey that "It 'tisn't customary" was her terrible indictment of those who were not so free.

It has become an old saw in the community that the sure way of having *the* last word in any discussion is to employ one of two magic formulae: (1) Sister Mechtilde's famous, "It 'tisn't customary"; or (2) "Mother Abbess said so." She who can lawfully employ one of these two has the undisputed Poor Clare peroration any time at all.

When a Poor Clare vows to live in obedience, her two hands are cradled in the hands of her abbess. It is a very beautiful and moving little gesture, but vastly significant, too. Each year of her life, a professed nun repeats that gesture when she kneels before the altar and privately renews her vows: "I again vow and promise God . . . and you, Mother . . ." Always that phrase: "And you, Mother". And always the daughter's hands laid in the hands of the mother. Sometimes, at renewals, the abbess is holding two slender young hands; sometimes, square, blunted hands; sometimes, gnarled old hands. But the beauty and significance remain unchanged: Here is my religious life which is willingly subject to your authority, which I entrust to your love and wisdom, which is yours to direct and sanctify, Mother.

How anyone can think that such submission demeans us is quite beyond me. Is there anything ignoble about the child who is sure that full security against all dangers is to be had by the simple expedient of placing its hands in the hands of its mother? And what do we get for such dependence? Nothing short of the certainty of an eternity of happiness. "And I", replies the abbess, "promise you, if you keep [observe] this, life everlasting." This is quite a promise for one mortal to make to another. Holy Church gives the abbess leave to make it, putting life everlasting, in a sense, into her hands to dispense to her daughters.

A Poor Clare abbess is a higher superior, that is, she has full rights over her subjects, and not just limited rights as superiors of active Orders have. This does not mean, of course, that she exercises the prerogative of putting her nuns "through the hoops". Contrariwise, St. Clare's admonitions to the abbess read like a breath out of Heaven. Whenever they are read in the refectory, I always hear, very distinctly, the swish of our Lady's mantle. There is so much of gentleness, of sweetness, and of love.

When I first heard our holy Rule read aloud, I was so charmed by the quaintness of its thirteenth-century phraseology that I missed most of its twentieth-century practicability. But two sentences struck me with great force; one, because it proved St. Clare was a poet; the other, because it proved that she put the ictus on the first word of the title "Mother Abbess".

At the end of her Testament, St. Clare writes: "I give you my blessing now while living, and after my death insofar as I may—nay, even more than I may!" Only a poet could make a promise like that. It would never be St. Clare to give only as much as she could give. The daughters of the future were not to receive less than the nuns at San Damiano, St. Clare would see to that. Was she not wed to One to whom miracles were the merest commonplace, and whose Divine Heart was even more extravagant than her own? "Nay, even more than I may!"

The other sentence that continued to sing in my heart for days and weeks after I first heard it was: "And I entreat her who shall be in office, that she strive to precede the other Sisters more by virtue and holy behavior, than by her office, so that, touched by her example, they obey her, not so much from a sense of duty, as from love." The grim tone of so many pious books which urge us to obey our superior however unlovable she may be by nature suggest that this is the normal cut of superiors. Such tomes cheer us on with dubiously joyous thoughts about all the warehousefuls of merits we are stacking up for ourselves by taking orders from someone for whom we feel a great aversion. The climax of all this would seem to be that you ought to pray to have an ogre as abbess; she would touch off your latent sanctity like a match set to a firecracker.

Of course, there is a wholesome truth at the bottom of all this, but it has been exaggerated out of all bounds. It is the business of the subject to obey her abbess whether she has any personal love for that dignitary or not. But it is not the business of the abbess to get a good grip on her authority and let love go by the board. St. Clare wants the abbesses of her Order to be leaders in virtue and superior to the other nuns in holy behavior. And when St. Clare sets down these norms, she shows how intensely practical and even shrewd she was. For mere authority as such never takes hold of our hearts, but virtue and holy lovableness do. We are directed in the ways of obedience by a lawful superior. We are led by a lovable one.

What puts the real twist into our hearts after our faults and small betrayals of grace but the aching knowledge that God loves us so tenderly and that we continue to disappoint and snub His love? Something of this carries over into our relations with our Mother Abbess. And, because of it, we are led very surely to God.

New postulants, with the starch of novelty thick upon them, usually address the abbess or refer to her as "Reverend Mother Abbess". It is significant that, after a few months, this becomes "Mother Abbess". And a postulant coming down the home stretch toward her investiture has invariably reduced the title to the sweet and simple one used by the professed nuns, "Mother". It is significant because it shows that a postulant has "got the feel" of the monastery, which is the home of a spiritual family whose sisterhood gathers warmth from the motherhood of its abbess. The title "Reverend Mother Abbess" is always used on formal occasions. For the rest, it is "Mother".

And to the abbess, each daughter is "child", from the seventeen-year-old postulant to the most rheumatic old aborigine in the infirmary. When I was a novice, Sister Evangela, after many praiseworthy attempts to die, which had all eventually come to nothing, seemed finally to be making the grade. At ninety, she lay in the infirmary, very cheerful in the hope that perhaps she was at last going to die, after all. (Sometimes, our more notoriously long-lived nuns get a little discouraged, like aged Sister Agatha, who used to sigh: "Well, I will die *some* day, that's sure.") Sister Evangela was old enough to have been Mother Abbess' grandmother, yet the abbess who fussed with the bedclothes and plumped the pillows and coaxed Sister Evangela to eat was waiting on her child and called her by that sweet name. It did not seem ludicrous, but only tender and completely right, that Mother should support the frail old body in her arms and ask: "Are you comfortable, child?"

Ancient Sister Evangela was as much Mother Abbess' child as were either of the two young postulants whom she discovered only this morning in the highest branches of our giant pecan-tree and summoned to her with a stricken: "Children, what are you doing up there?" Two dark curly heads peered down at her. "Dear Mistress told us to pick the pecans. Some are 'way up here." Here was a kind of literal obedience that appealed strongly to postulant hearts! And a fine consideration for most high poverty was evinced by their carefully hanging their little black veils on a low branch before shinnying up into pecan-stratosphere.

The intimacy of the cloister brings out the maternal coloring of the abbess' position in full tones. Everything stems from her, from an aspirin for the cold in your head to a mother's ear for the problem in your heart. And the closeness of a monastic family is more clearly exemplified by the very old than by the very young. The veteran Poor Clares are, by a marvelous paradox, both toughened and mellowed by a lifetime of obedience. Yet, as their dim old eyes begin to catch a rumorous glimpse of eternity, they feel more than ever the attitude of a child toward its mother. This is, I think, one of the very beautiful rewards of obedience.

Sister Mechtilde and Sister Evangela were contemporaries, and Sister Evangela was a bit testy about the fact that she required chauffeuring about in a wheelchair, whereas Sister Mechtilde—young scamp—could still fend for herself with a cane. Sister Evangela blamed this unfair circumstance entirely on the fact that the young nuns waxed the monastery floors too heavily. "Too greasy", she would complain in her high little voice. "I could walk as well as the next one" (and everyone knew whom she very particularly meant by "the next one") "if they didn't make the floors so greasy." However, Sister Evangela worsted Sister Mechtilde in the valiant contest to die. Sister Mechtilde had to stomp about without her boon companion for two years after Sister Evangela had triumphantly got out of that wheelchair to walk to Heaven.

The obedience of lovable old veterans like these is an open spiritual book in which the novices and young nuns can read to their profit. To these dear ancients belongs, above all the others, the title of proved child of God and of the Mother Abbess.

It is our custom to present any pieces of finished work to Mother Abbess for her approval or criticism. All such monastic customs run in the very bloodstream of the old nuns, and I remember often hearing the infirmarian ask Mother Abbess to come to the infirmary at some odd time because "Sister Mechtilde would like to show her work." Sister would be propped up in bed, mending someone's undergarments with great clumsy patches and generous stitches. But this was all the work she could do now. And so it must be shown to Mother Abbess. Foolish? Oh, no! The young nun writing books or painting canvases in oils may perhaps be doing something far less important in God's eyes than is the old child in the infirmary patching under-tunics.

This is another of the marvels of living in obedience.

No one is ever doing anything more important than you are, if you are obeying. A broom, a pen, a needle are all the same to God. The obedience of the hand that plies them and the love in the heart of the nun who holds them are what make an eternal difference to God, to the nuns, and to all the world.

Still another wonder of this living in obedience is the juxtaposing of the mother–child relationship not only with ease but sometimes with most poignant sweetness, as when the aged abbess in Chicago, at last unable to fulfill the duties of her position as abbess or vicaress any longer, was succeeded by our present abbess, whom she had received as a postulant, clothed as a novice, and whose hands she had held at the profession of vows. Now the child was the Mother Abbess and the aged ex-abbess was the happy child who struggled out of the infirmary bed to ask the blessing of one whom she had blessed so many hundreds of times, and then died contentedly in the arms of her former postulant.

When Mother Abbess renews her holy vows each October, I always feel a little sorry for her. She has no one's hands to cradle her own. She begins her formula of renewals with the same words: "I again vow and promise God . . ." but she cannot complete it with the tenderly warm addition: "and you, Mother". And no one promises her life everlasting when she finishes speaking. I should say I used to feel sorry for her, before I developed more acute monastic hearing. Now, my heart picks up the response very clearly, when St. Clare makes it. She wanted the abbesses who succeeded her in office to be such that the other nuns could obey them, "not so much from a sense of duty, as from love". When the abbess can command that sort of obedience from her monastic children, St. Clare herself promises her life everlasting.

How do I know? Why, I heard her, only last October.

8 BUT MARTHA SERVED

For our Lord Himself placed us so that we should be, by our manner of living, a model and a mirror, not only for all the faithful, but for our own Sisters also.

—TESTAMENT OF ST. CLARE

Of late, cloistered nuns themselves have come to be just as wrongly envisioned as their active Sisters. Paradoxically, the current flare-up of interest in the monastic Orders, with all its attendant mass of literature, is also a current smoldering of confused and erroneous notions. Too many persons have become heated in trying to prove that active Sisters are doing far more for God than the contemplatives. And too many other persons have worked themselves into a mental lather declaring that contemplative nuns go the "whole way" for God, whereas active Sisters stop at the halfway mark. This is indeed a sad state of affairs, for active Sisters and contemplative nuns form a single and marvelous entity, not two hostile camps.

Contemplative nuns have been labeled as useless, parasitical, shiftless, for centuries. But we just do not run a temperature over it. What does it matter if some people think that the Church needs only active Sisters and that contemplatives should be "liberated"; and that other people think that active Sisters are just spiritual sluggards? What matters is what God thinks. And God will scarcely ask His contemplatives to sally forth into the world, or blame His apostles for not dwelling in cloisters. The Spirit breatheth where He will. And haloes will most likely continue to be evenly distributed by the angels in charge to teachers, nurses, social service workers, and contemplatives.

Perhaps I can claim a certain advantage in writing of active and contemplative religious, because I first entered an active Congregation, spending two fruitful and memory-treasured years as a candidate of the School Sisters of Notre Dame. Leaving their motherhouse was the hardest thing I had ever done in my life. It seemed that my heart was being torn up by the roots when I took my last long look at that beloved sprawling building set on the slope-shouldered hill. And the notion that I could have thought I was doing something greater than these wonderful Sisters when I left them to enter a cloister is so fantastically impossible that I lack all words of befitting anathema for it!

A vocation is so mysterious a gift, a thing so locked in the inner court of the soul, where alone God speaks His wishes, that no one can properly describe or explain it. What can be said is that a true vocation is a call so compelling that a soul must loosen its hold on the dearest and even the holiest of its loves to rise up and follow the summons. Once, a higher superior asked me why I had become a Poor Clare. I would have liked to die at that moment! For one can scarcely stand up before strange priests and dignitaries and say: "I don't really know. I was the happiest active Order postulant in the world, preparing for a life of the teaching which I loved. But then God said: 'Go!' and I went."

Of course, I admit to being a bit prejudiced in favor of active Sisters because of the fact that the School Sisters of Notre Dame who educated me, loved and guided and inspired me, were truly God's gentlewomen. They must have known long before I myself knew that I really wanted to be one of them. Looking back on the days when I would torture them by tagging after them long after school hours were over, dropping in on them early and late, and once growing mildly ecstatic over being permitted to share their recreation hour, I can visualize the smiles I never saw at the time. When I was twelve years old, one of them became the most potent factor in my life in helping me to define my ideals and set my future course. Across many miles and with no need of words, Sister Mary Noreen remains in my life that same potent factor.

People have sometimes said to me: "What a pity you wasted two years before you found your real vocation." Wasted! The two years I spent with the Notre Dame Sisters taught me lessons of the spiritual life that I shall never forget. Those years were part of my real vocation, for they prepared me for the cloister. Best of all, they gave me an intimate appreciation of the glorious life of a religious teacher and a realization of how the active and contemplative vocations are intended by God to be, now no longer two, but one in a single Love and in a complete service of that Love.

If I understood dimly on the day I left the School Sisters of Notre Dame that I was helping to fulfill their vocation by becoming a contemplative, their own spiritual wisdom knew it comprehensively. When they were sure I was sure, they helped me in every possible way. They gave me their warmest shawls because they feared the monastery would be cold. The candidates' Mistress hoped that my new Mistress would not let me exhaust myself: "*You* never know when you're tired!" One very old Sister worried that I would find it difficult to adjust to the new life: "You know, my dear, they use *colored* handkerchiefs!" They took me to the railway station and would have accompanied me all the way to the monastery had I not vigorously protested the expense and time involved for those busy Sisters. They permitted me to wear their own candidate's dress and black-veiled bonnet to the monastery to spare me the sorrow of changing to secular clothes again. And one after another of them sealed a little agreement with me: they would teach for me, and I would dwell enclosed for them. Together, our lives would be one life.

On my investiture day, Mother Abbess added to my name the title "of our Lady". "I wanted you to feel that you still belong to Notre Dame", she said to me afterward. And she smiled. Mother Abbess, too, educated by the School Sisters and herself nearly one of them, loved their Congregation with all her heart. Do you wonder, after all this, that all of us get spiritual indigestion from literature which suggests there are "strained relations" between active and contemplative Orders?

Last summer, at the University of Notre Dame, Sisters of eleven different active Congregations played roles in the play I had been invited to write by the head of the speech department there. And they proved that the love and veneration of active Sisters for contemplative religious is not at all confined to the one Congregation I knew so well. The Sisters tape-recorded *Domitille*. They sent pictures of every scene. They wrote notes and letters, and did everything short of coming to Roswell to perform it for us at the grille. They probably would have done that, too, if they could have. In fact, we were all amused over the one thing that nettled the Sisters about the play. Domitille, the cloistered nun on whom the play turns, was not exactly an engaging character. She did not "convert" in the final scene. The Sisters would have none of this! The cloistered heroine must be a heroine in the best edifying style. And so they insisted that Domitille do an about-face in the last scene. It spoiled the sense of the play, but it placated the Sisters, who wanted nothing untoward hinted of any cloistered nun.

Our Lord Himself, by one of those gracious courtesies for which He has become universally celebrated, elected to evince His divine pleasure in the cooperation of contemplative nuns and active Sisters in producing *Domitille* by a rather singular turn of events. Had I been asked to choose from all those of my acquaintance the one most eminently qualified to interpret the demanding role of Veronica in the play, I would have selected the poet whose lovely songs have stirred so many hearts, Sister M. Maura, S.S.N.D. But Sister Maura was in Baltimore, and the play would be produced in South Bend by summer students in the playwriting class of Dr. Natalie White. A mere nothing, the Lord seemed to say!

So the Holy Spirit whispered to Sister Maura's superior that what Sister should do is go to the University of Notre Dame and study playwriting. Then He told Dr. White to cast Sister as Veronica. Then He said to me: "Anything else, Sister Francis?" I could think of nothing. I could only remember Hilaire Belloc's writing of the graciousness of the Child Jesus: "He was so small you could not see/ His large intent of courtesy." Now, in His manhood, it has become very evident.

When Martha served, our dear Lord found no fault with her. She was rendering Him a very perfect service in the vocation to which she was called. It was only when she turned an accusing eye on Mary that our Lord rebuked her. So it will be for anyone foolish enough to blame a contemplative for not "doing something useful" or to censure an active religious for not "going all the way". A contemplative nun praying and doing penance is doing the most useful thing in the world, without which no amount of Catholic Action would accomplish anything at all. An active Sister wearing out her strength and her life on Christ's members has assuredly gone all the way. Our Lord *is* the Way. And all religious, active or contemplative, go by that same Way to learn the Truth which He also is and to gain the eternal Life which is likewise Himself.

Here in Roswell, the problems of our nursing Sisters are our own problems. They tell us of each stage of their new hospital building project because they realize it is important to us and that we try to help build the new wing with our prayers and sacrifices. In turn, they interest themselves in all our material needs, and a Poor Clare who must be hospitalized in Roswell is assured of the most tender and devoted care from loving hospital Sisters. It was the same when we were in Chicago.

Any true religious surely knows that she never succeeds in "going all the way" for God. She only tries. And would any religious dare or care to say: None has done more than I! The best contemplative nun is the one who carries the whole world and its spiritual interests in her heart, and the best active Sister is the one who keeps enclosure of the heart.

As mentioned before, the masters of the spiritual life have always concurred on the best spiritual tape measure of a religious: his or her regard for the contemplative state. We have been privileged to have some of the greatest national figures of our day as personal friends of our community, men and women whose lives teem with activity and whose reverence for the contemplative life is unbounded.

The late Father Daniel A. Lord, S.J., seemed to touch bottom on the tenderness of his great heart when he spoke or wrote of contemplatives. Kathleen and Rosemary, the first two postulants to enter the Roswell cloister, learned of us from Father Lord, and he rejoiced in their vocations like the proud spiritual father he was.

That great and gracious lady Sister M. Madeleva, C.S.C., wrote to Mother Abbess: "How I rejoice that this gift of poetry is secure in the cloister." She encouraged me to write, she smoothed rough edges off our poetry with her own beautiful wisdom and sensitive feeling for beauty, and she wrote her name in recommendation across our first published collection of poems. On a bitterly cold November day, she made the long trip to the monastery and sat at the parlor grille with the rapt attention of one who had come to learn. My uncle, who had chauffeured her from her lecture engagement to the monastery, said to me afterward: "She has a deeply spiritual face." I rejoined: "And a soul to match." I have always felt a deeply personal satisfaction in the title literary critics have conferred on dear Sister Madeleva: "The lady abbess of nun poets".

Hilaire Belloc's granddaughter is a cloistered nun, a Canoness of St. Augustine. When that grand old man sent his daughter, Eleanor Jebb, to visit our monastery to deliver his message that "These poems set bells ringing in my heart", he also sent her with the message of his own esteem for contemplatives. "I visit my daughter through a grille just like this," smiled the charming Mrs. Jebb, "and we try to match our eyes to the same opening!" She added later: "My father is very holy in his old age. He hopes so much for your prayers." It was wonderful to hear her reminisce of "deah Gilbert and deah Frahnces", but more wonderful (because more humbling) to see the regard of the prodigiously active Belloc—"God's gunner", as Father Vincent McNabb liked to call him—and his daughter for the cloistered contemplatives. They knew that contemplatives try to direct with prayer to the target of souls the missiles of all God's gunners.

Cardinal Mercier bewailed the fact that some priests seem to deplore the disappearance of rare souls and greatly talented young people into cloisters. The idea of deploring rather than applauding such disappearances startled the great Cardinal out of his habitual reserve of speech. "Good heavens", he ejaculated. "What would become of us all without the contemplatives!"

Bishop Raymond A. Lane of Maryknoll told us how, when he was laboring out on distant missions, he often felt what seemed like a real physical force holding him back from his labors, especially when a group of pagans was to be baptized. At such moments, the Bishop said, he would quickly renew in his heart the recommendation of himself and his work to the cloistered nuns whose prayers he had asked. The diabolic force that held him would then unfailingly be shattered, like locks sprung on heavy chains. Our bond with Maryknoll is, incidentally, as strong as it is treasured, on both sides.

Activity not rooted in prayer is mere bombast and flurry. It may raise a great deal of dust and deafen many an ear, but it will never make a dent on things eternal. Activity which takes its strength from prayer and which looks to contemplatives to fill up its measure, just as contemplatives look to God's infantry to satisfy the burning missionary drive in their own hearts, will have God Himself for its eternal monument.

When Father James Keller writes: "I count on the Poor Clares to put our Christopher television program over", he is merely being practical. He is not crediting the Poor Clares. He is crediting prayer and God's word. So is Monsignor Thomas Little, who asks us to help Catholics be loyal to their National Legion of Decency pledge by our prayers. So are the university presidents begging the prayerful support of the cloistered nuns for their vast duties, as much as the mothers worrying over Jimmie's poor grades in school. People usually enclose an alms in these letters as another evidence of their practical view of contemplatives; they feel they want to help feed and clothe the nuns to whom their problems are personal problems and who are trying to resolve those problems with their prayers and sacrifices. But alms or no alms, they get the prayers and the sacrifices.

It would not be necessary to consider at such length the superficial comparisons of the active and contemplative religious life, made by persons who understand neither, when thoughtful men and women so manifestly appreciate how the one complements the other, were it not for the fact of so many popular misconceptions arising from those unjustifiable comparisons. One of the most widespread of these misconceptions concerns the matter of education.

Recently, we were reading in our refectory a currently popular book about the religious life. We were enjoying it immensely, chuckling over the authentic conventual atmosphere of the writing and rejoicing in the homespun spirituality of it. Then we got a most unpleasant surprise. The heads of the older nuns jerked up in amazement, and the postulants wriggled indignantly on their benches. For the author had begun to discourse on education and its present-day necessity— "*except* in cloisters, where it is of no particular use". No matter how widespread this false notion is, it never fails to rouse us!

Now, it is scarcely flattering to the Almighty to consider that His "garden enclosed" is peopled with those unequipped for any active apostolate. Neither does such an attitude indicate a real understanding of the meaning of education. In an age of specialists, like ours, where so many persons know a great deal about one thing and nothing about everything, the true meaning of education is well on the way to being lost.

It is true that if one's notion of an educated girl is a walking warehouse stocked ceiling-high with facts, her kind of "education" may be quite useless in the cloister. It will be as useless here as it will be anywhere else, except perhaps on one of those information-quiz-fizz radio or television programs where she may win a few thousand dollars because she knows that George Eliot was really Mary Ann Evans, though she would be hard put to draw on the philosophy of old Silas Marner and relate it to any others of her assorted facts.

Education worthy of the name is built on integration and correlation of knowledge. It has nothing at all to do with the ability to spout facts like a geyser. Real education brings to flower the seeds of intelligence in the human mind. Intelligence is quite independent of education, it is true (one of the most intelligent women I ever knew was also one of the most unschooled), but education is a cultivation of the intelligence; and the blossoms it produces are just as fragrant in the cloister as anywhere else, and just as necessary. Thus, we require a high school education and consider a college education highly desirable.

A truly educated girl is equipped to draw on her own resources. She is trained in the schools to hold correct perspectives on life and is keen to discern the true from the merely specious. She has mental poise and a certain mental maturity which is at once the condition and the reward of the integrating and correlating of knowledge. She is more humble because of her education than she would be without it. True education always fosters humility, although mere accumulation of facts fosters pride. All these things are requisite in the cloister. Above all, authentic education fits a person for a life of solitude. A girl who has learned to cultivate the soil of her own intelligence is already conditioned for an interior life. Her education is thus supremely useful to her in the cloister.

A cloistered nun who has been trained to relate one science to another will ordinarily be quicker to relate the unfolding mysteries of the spiritual life one to another, and also to recognize the superb paradox on which the interior life is built and in which all these mysteries discover their integrity: humility is exaltation, effacement is enrichment, death is life, and all the other facets of the one splendrous truth which is Love. A cultivated mind is accustomed to cut its way through mere excrescences to the core of things, and this aptitude is of utmost importance in the enclosed contemplative life, where one can so easily get lost in a clutter of inconsequentials and mistake a scratch on the epidermis for a mortal wound.

The Poor Clares are not scanning the vocation horizon for Ph.D.'s; but if a postulant holds one, so much the better. For, all of this is not to say that our monasteries are houses of study, but only that a real education is supremely useful in the cloister. And we modify education always with the searching adjective "real".

I like to remember the point a good friend of ours, a Trappist monk, scored when he said that the urchin who leans out of his tenement window and whistles sharply with an appreciative: "Hey, Maggie, lookit de stars!— dey're t'ick as bedbugs!" is more truly educated than some pint-sized Park Avenue pedant who can perhaps quote some pertinent lines from *Romeo and Juliet* about stars, but with that complete lack of feeling and deep understanding peculiar to pedants, whether budding or full-blown. The urchin, after all, is drawing on his own resources. He is educing a comment from the mine of his own intelligence. And he is very neatly, if unbeautifully, correlating one fact to another!

As for the skills a girl may have acquired in the process of being educated, these will almost unfailingly be put to good use in the cloister. If occasionally they are not, then they can be used in the most perfect sense of all: for a sacrifice. However, a girl with a true vocation never worries about that side of the question, even though it is a matter of record that no graduate nurse is unwelcome in a cloister infirmary, or musician at the organ, or teacher in chant class, or stenographer at the typewriter. Even the former beautician will very likely be invited to wave and curl the postulants' hair for their investiture days!

Anything given with complete trust into the hands of God, without any care for His choice or disposal, is already used to perfection. St. Clare knew this so well when St. Francis led her to draughty old San Damiano and she placed her passionate love of music, her intense regard for learning, and the whole beauty-thirsty fabric of her character and personality on the little altar there. She never took them off that altar, being always content to let God either use her or simply accept her, as He desired.

In *The Legend and Writings of St. Clare of Assisi*, published by the Franciscan Institute of America, Father Ignatius Brady, O.F.M., and Sister Mary Frances, S.M.I.C., have beautifully clarified St. Clare's concept of the contemplative life, which was built on the doctrine of the Mystical Body as on a rock. She would not recognize as her daughter a Poor Clare enclosed in the stuffy quarters of her own spiritual life. As a matter of fact, any spiritual life which does not embrace the whole Mystical Body has never even grown strong enough to walk about in stuffy quarters. It suffocated in the womb. Those who dote on the precious little pictures stocked in pious shops, the kind in which you see the religious, long hair and draperies trailing, skipping daintily from step to step on the way to her own perfection, the inevitable lily dangling from one hand, would be more than startled by St. Clare's language when she describes the life of her Poor Ladies.

"Servants", "co-workers", "a support to the weak and frail members of Christ's Mystical Body"—these are the terms which recur again and again. She wants her nuns to be "sacrificial victims, holy and pleasing to God". The spiritual service of God in a life of voluntary and continual self-sacrifice is the dominating and characteristic element of the Order she founded. And by this spiritual service, she intended that her daughters should be "shining lights and bright mirrors of perfection for those in the world", as she wrote in her Testament.

St. Clare knew perfectly the role of the contemplative in a world of action, and the part of the active apostle in the world of the spirit. When St. Francis doubted whether he himself should not lead an entirely contemplative life, he asked his cloistered daughter's advice. And St. Clare's answer came to him from the heart of her own enclosed life of prayer: No! St. Francis was to preach the word of God in the marketplace, to trudge the roads of the world and set men's hearts on fire with love. From her cloister, St. Clare would give unction to his words by her prayer, and strike off from the flint of her sacrifice the fire for his torch. That is why St. Francis is acknowledged by all to be one of the greatest and purest contemplatives who ever lived, and why St. Clare was such a prodigious missionary. They must be baffled in Heaven by the controversies of our age over the active and contemplative life. But when they consult Divine Wisdom about this strange state of affairs, I think God only smiles.

9 "WHAT DO THEY DO ALL DAY?"

*Let the Sisters to whom the Lord has given the grace of working,
labor faithfully and devotedly after the hour of Terce.*

—RULE OF ST. CLARE

When our present Novice Mistress was a young nun just
sufficiently seasoned in monastic life to have thought she
knew all possible parental objections to the Poor Clare
way of life, as well as all parental queries about the same,
and happy in the surety that God had well supplied all
the required answers, her mother came to visit her.
Mama was a staunch Irish Catholic and had harbored no
real objections to her daughter's vocation at any time. In
fact, she rather gloried in it. She suffered only that vague
sense of bewilderment that the cloistered contemplative
life occasions for so many.

Mama was thoroughly convinced of her girl's happiness by this time and firm in her belief that a vocation to
the cloistered life was the greatest privilege God could
give any girl. Her theory was sound. But the practice
puzzled Mama. She could no longer guard the burning
question, and it flared out this day at the parlor grille:
"Darling, what do you do all day?"

The contemplative life looks like a leisurely affair to most persons. The nuns chant the Divine Office and pray privately, and they—er—well, what do they do? How do they fill in time, of which they must certainly have vast commodities? Sister Regina, who had come puffing into the monastery parlor from one last task which simply had to be finished before the visit, stared at her mother in dumbfounded amazement. Mama felt she must have said something out of place, so she amended her query with an even more unfortunate question: "What I mean is, dear, how do you all manage to keep busy in there?" This was too much for Sister Regina. She laughed hard and long, while Mama looked first disconcerted and then amused in an uncomprehending sort of way. No one could resist joining in laughter as spontaneous as that! When the merriment finally calmed down to an explanation of how the nuns "fill in time", Mama was bewildered in an entirely new sense. Her new query became: "How can you do all that in one day?"

Not long after midnight a nun who may happen to be awake, for some strange reason not common among Poor Clares, will hear the warning summons of Sister Sacristan's alarm clock. When that dignitary has gathered her wits sufficiently to shut the thing off, she sets her jaw for what is at once a beautiful and a grim task: to rouse all the other sleeping nuns. It is a beautiful task because the Sacristan's bell is summoning the community to a midnight tryst with God. It is a grim business because Poor Clares unfortunately carry their souls about in the same clay casing found on the rest of humanity. Consequently, though the soul is ready and waiting to go to the choir and begin the chants of the night Office, the flesh finds the idea not at all stimulating. That is why the night Office is a cloistered nun's greatest privilege and joy and also her greatest external penance. That is also why the night Office is so precious in the sight of God.

Once you get "Brother Ass" standing, things begin to take shape in the mists of your mind. You remember what feast it is, and you start gathering all the sinning and suffering world into your heart as you make your sleepy way to the choir. Poor Clares observe the ancient monastic custom of sleeping fully garbed, which not only simplifies night rising but also endows even their sleep with beauty and significance. Our Lord has warned us that we know neither the day nor the hour when death will come like a thief in the night. A cloistered daughter of St. Francis is garbed in all her monastic livery whenever this welcome thief chooses to break the locks on her life. Like the wise virgins who heard the shout at midnight: "Behold, the bridegroom cometh! Go ye forth to meet him!" she is ready in her bridal dress to meet her Bridegroom. And, in a very practical sense, sleeping in the full monastic garb is a great advantage when all one's powers of concentration are needed to sweep the cobwebby sleep from one's mind. All a Poor Clare need do, as far as apparel is concerned, when she hears the Matins bell, is to spring up, tighten her cord, and throw her choir veil over her head to replace the short veil worn in bed.

Postulants are greatly handicapped by the lack of a monastic habit. Sleeping in nightgowns, they are obliged to dress for the occasion. And many a postulant who has staggered sleepily to Matins wearing her cape inside out, or trailing clouds of her Communion-veil glory, longs for the holy habit for more reasons than one.

Once you arrive in the choir, where our Lord waits exposed in the Blessed Sacrament, the full beauty of the night Office takes hold of your heart and soul. The chantress intones a hymn proper to the feast and then the great Office of the Church for the new day begins. When I was a postulant, I used to thrill to the sound of the nuns' voices chanting an invitation to all creation: "*Venite, adoremus!*"—"Oh, come, let us adore!" I still thrill to the utter rightness of it each dark morning anew.

Blackness clings to the great, tall windows in the choir, and the huge grille over the altar reaches long fingers of shadow down toward the chanting nuns. The electric lights directly above the heads of the choristers do not dispel the nocturnal dark of the choir, through which the voices of the nuns cut clean paths of praise and adoration, love and thanksgiving. It is at once the most magnificent and the most intimate of the canonical hours. Magnificent, because the surging chants of Matins are washing up waves of light on the dark shores of the world long before little Brother Sun has lifted his torch in the sleeping skies. Intimate, because the secrecy and mystery of night hold the Sacramental Christ and the chanting nuns in a close embrace.

All the petitions for which we have been asked to pray are gathered into these morning songs of holy Church. And all the anguish and loneliness and fear of those who have never heard of us and of whom we have never heard are gathered, too. I always feel, at the night Office, that we are walking down all the avenues of the universe, lighting God's lamps on every corner.

The nun who goes back to her cell after Matins may be tired, but she is the happiest person in the world. From entering the choir and prostrating before the Blessed Sacrament, through raising a dry-throated song to God and then begging Him in a solemn prayer to "Open her mouth to bless His holy Name", right down to the last "Amen", she has been busy at the only really important thing any human being has to do. She will work, later in the day, giving her hands and her mind to many tasks; but these first hours of the day which is still as young as night are sacrosanct for the work which will occupy all of us throughout all eternity. That is why there is such a sense of satisfaction about the night Office. We press our foreheads to the floor and say: "*Adoramus Te!*"—"We adore Thee!" We trace the sign of the Cross on our lips to seal them for a new day's praise of God. We rise and kneel and chant to worship Him. For this, all of us were born, and for nothing else.

Who knows how many chasms of sin are leaped, how many hatreds wilt, how much anguish is softened and consecrated in the world because some have stepped out of the world to begin the work of eternity beforehand? This is the great mystery of God's love, by which no credit accrues to contemplatives, but all glory returns to Him Who owns it.

There is another short period of sleep after Matins until Sister Sacristan again takes bell in hand and peals out the message that it is time for Lauds. Now there are full morning ablutions to perform, day habits and Communion guimpes and veils to don; and there soon follows a great scampering of the junior division to the choir to get the stalls dusted before Mother Abbess arrives to begin the morning Office.

Soon after I entered the monastery, the Novice Mistress had me sufficiently impressed with the responsibility of the postulants to get the choir dusted before morning prayer, and never to permit the old nuns (some of whom were notorious early-arrivers in the choir) to do that chore. I was ablaze with zeal! I took the dormitory stairs like a March wind, slid into the choir on one black-slippered foot, and made for the desk where the blue checkered choir dusters awaited me. But, no! There was old Sister Bernard with a blue duster in her hand! I scampered over to her choir stall, beamed, and made her the sign to give me the duster. This seemed to amaze Sister Bernard no little. I repeated the sign more carefully. Maybe I had not got it just right before. Sister Bernard leaned forward slightly and peered at me in the manner of one examining a very curious object. But she kept hold of the duster.

I was getting desperate. The nuns were beginning to file in at the back doors of the choir, with my side of choir still undusted. Mabel was efficiently finishing up the other side with the duster she had taken from the desk. My responsibility was heavy upon me, and the thought of Dear Mistress' imminent arrival gave me the determination that decides the fate of nations. I gave Sister Bernard an apologetic smile and yanked the duster out of her hand. Only it wasn't a duster. It was her handkerchief.

It required quite some explaining from the Novice Mistress to convince staid Sister Bernard that the new postulant was not completely mad. In fact, it was never recorded and witnessed that she *was* convinced.

When the aged teaching Sister worried about those "colored handkerchiefs" I would have to use as a Poor Clare, she little dreamed where my true handkerchief trial would lie. We postulants had smallish handkerchiefs, and I was still too uninured to monastic ways to suspect that the handkerchiefs affected by the novices and professed nuns were the size of young tablecloths.

When the last veil has fluttered into choir, Mother Abbess begins the short morning prayer which precedes Lauds. Again, all the intentions of friends and benefactors and the needs of the whole world are offered up like a chalice of tears to a compassionate God. Lauds itself is sheer poetry, from the glorious cadences of its opening hymn, through the tremendous plea: "O Christ, Son of the living God, have mercy on us!", to the final petition that God will show quick mercy to the souls in Purgatory and bring them into the rest which He is.

In the midst of Lauds, the versicular leaves her stall and goes to the lectern to call the roll of the saints of the next day. It is kind of liturgical preview of the next showing, but has a thunder and a glory all its own. On the greatest solemnities, two candle-bearer novices stand beside the versicular, and the announcement of the next feast is chanted with all possible solemnity.

On Easter morning, when my first monastic Holy Week had prepared me for the full meaning of the Resurrection, I wondered how there could be a proper word for Easter. Even Christmas has its poignancy; but Easter is joy so pure, so blinding, that it throws the heart down as surely as it felled those guards at His tomb. But then the high, sweet voice of the old nun sang out: "On this day the solemnity of all solemnities". Two white-veiled novices stood at either side of the lectern, like the angels of the Resurrection. And I knew that was the word for it: Solemnity of all solemnities; crown of all feasts, climax of all mysteries, peak of all joys.

On Christmas Eve, it was a young nun who sang the moving announcement of Christ's Birth, beginning with the creation of the world and carefully measuring the lessening years in the rising cadences of the exquisite melody until her fresh young voice had traveled down to Bethlehem and the year from which all years take their places as being before or after. Then we all fell on our knees while the singing voice rose to the simple statement of the miracle which was the beginning of our redemption: the Nativity of our Lord Jesus Christ according to the flesh. The young voice halted its song, and absolute silence hung like a cloud of wonder over the choir. The meaning of Christmas became very clear, and I was not embarrassed to be brushing away grateful tears. So many others were doing the same.

There is a half hour of meditation after Lauds, followed by Terce, that part of the Office which summons the Holy Spirit upon the new day and is our immediate preparation for the holy sacrifice of the Mass. Mass has an entirely new significance for the heart which has been prepared for it by the Divine Office. Beginning with the night Office of Matins, you have gradually become saturated with the spiritual joy of the day's feast or the grave beauty of the feria. Now comes the great and climactic sacrifice for which your soul has been well briefed. The conventual Mass is the great event in the monastic day. To it, all things lead, and from it all others progress.

In the autumn of 1954, we had flash floods throughout most of New Mexico. Torrents of water poured down from the mountains, washing out homes and taking a toll of several lives. There was one morning when our chaplain could not get through to the monastery for holy Mass. It was an immeasurable loss, but it was also a tremendous grace; for it gave us a very practical realization of what the day is without holy Mass. We wandered about, that vague morning, groping for a schedule that had suddenly become quite meaningless since it flowed from no wellspring. The soul had fled from the day and left us with a dead body of hours. Next morning, when Father somehow accomplished the feat of breasting the waters in our driveway, we felt we were re-entering our own lives from which we had temporarily been shut out.

A nun too ill to leave the infirmary for holy Mass has the same experience. Everything becomes unreal and she cannot quite get hold of her life or the day. Both are unhinged. And this sense of loss and deprivation can make her suffering as effective as it is affective.

The conventual Mass is often followed by Benediction. I swing down the long lane of the choir from our own stall to the sanctuary, unpinning our long enclosure veil and doffing our mantle en route. There will be no opportunity to blame mistakes at the organ on arms weighted down by a mantle or fingers catching in the folds of an enclosure veil! I calculate the needed length of the organ prelude by quick glances at the altar grille, through whose thin curtain I can glimpse the circumlocutions of very small altar boys lighting very tall candles.

Then Father lifts the monstrance with its precious Burden up onto the throne. Christ in His ring of jeweled gold looks down on us. Christ so newly come into our hearts looks back. This is the moment I love, the moment which signifies for me the embrace of the Father and the Son. I intone the *O Salutaris Hostia*, very happy on the little plain of the organ bench with the forest of my singing Sisters all around me, and waiting for the imminent blessing of the Divine Carpenter upon us and all who will work this day in His name.

The period of private thanksgiving after holy Mass and Benediction is followed by the community's corporate invocation of the Holy Spirit upon the day's work. Our Blessed Mother is summoned to lend her love and protection to our toil, and the blessing of our holy

Mother St. Clare is asked. This last impressed me deeply when I was a new recruit in the monastic corps. The prayer to our foundress ends: "Bestow on us, one and all, thy maternal benediction." And all the nuns immediately make the sign of the Cross, receiving the blessing. Here is faith. No one for a moment doubts that the spirit of our beloved Mother St. Clare arches like a smile over the big choir. No one supposes that a mother who is asked for her blessing does not immediately give it. All make the sign of the Cross and then leave the choir with the happy assurance of souls that have seen the hand of their mother uplifted in blessing.

This seems to me to be part of our Franciscan heritage. It is that same hard practicality that nettled the world in St. Francis and St. Clare. If you ask a blessing of God, you get it; ask and receive, He said. If you want to be perfect, you go and sell whatever you have and follow the Lord. If you want to be forgiven by your Father in Heaven, you forgive your brethren on earth. All very simple. And very disconcerting to those who are not so simple.

Breakfast is a brief affair of bread and coffee. The most important thing about it is that the abbess now subjoins her blessing to that of St. Clare. "Dear Sisters, may God grant you a good day. Begin your work with the blessing of God." This stirring monastic form of "good morning" is repeated in chorus by all the kneeling nuns. "Reverend Mother Abbess and holy community, may God grant you a good day." You have a good feeling in the heart, too. Since the short period of sleep following the night Office, you have again given your full and undivided attention to God from 5:10 until 7:30. You have every reason to believe that this day, as all monastic days, will indeed be a good day. Its firstfruits were given to God and consecrated for His use. It only remains to see what mysteries of His love and grace will unfold before you in this fresh day. Every day lived for God is a rare adventure. And a Poor Clare nun feels this strongly when she leaves the refectory each morning, in soul refreshed with many blessings, and in body fortified with hot coffee and homemade bread.

Now the big monastery stretches its long cloisters like arms, the windows yawn wide with sunlight, and sounds and smells awaken everywhere. Soon the fragrant odor of cooking apples and baking bread comes spiraling out of the kitchen. Typewriters begin their tap dance. Suppressed giggles drift through the windows on the west side, where the postulants are dragging yard-long roots of Bermuda grass out of the field so that the harassed peas and squash can get through. The sacristan goes to see about the Lord's accessories for His next public appearance. A sewing machine begins to hum to the tune of someone's new choir mantle. The portress comes from the turn with a broad grin and a gallon of—ice cream! A benefactor has remembered with ice cream that this day is the anniversary of our coming to Roswell.

The silence that pervades the monastery during the time of work is a quiet full of busy sounds. And in the works of the different nuns, the liturgy itself takes on sounds and smells. If you hear the novices' tremulous solfeggio of the last poignant responsories of Advent, and your feet start dancing to the charming pastorals the organist is practicing in the library, you remind your heart that the sands of Advent are almost run out into Christmas. If you smell sauerkraut, you know it is a vigil; but if you smell asparagus, you have a proof of a great feast-day as well as a reminder to thank God that the asparagus crop in the back garden was so abundant this year.

The hum of work ceases at eleven o'clock, when the Offices of Sext and None are chanted. Again the monastery sinks down contentedly into the bosom of God, its whole life regathered into the chanting voices of the nuns. If it is summer, you come into the cool shadows of the choir with your garden habit damp against your back and your sunburned bare feet grateful for the coldness of the bare wood floor. In winter, you take up your breviary into red and roughened hands and let your soul enjoy the warmth of God's Sacramental Presence.

Sext and None were St. Clare's favorite canonical hours, for they are especially commemorative of the crucifixion and death of our blessed Lord. She would often chant Sext and None with the tears streaming down her cheeks, so perfectly was her seraphic heart attuned to the mysteries of the sacred Passion. "O God unchangeable and true", we sing out in the hymn of None; and the sorrows of the crucifixion are at once heightened and sweetened in our souls by that glorious exclamation which affirms the stability of monastic life

founded on the vast unchangeableness of God and rewarded by the truth of His promises.

This Office chanted, consciences looked into and
burnished, and prayers said for the benefactors whose
charity provides for our needs, we go to dinner, chanting in the procession that magnificent psalm "*Miserere
mei, Deus!*"—"Have mercy on me, O God!"—which is
proof enough that David was indeed inspired. There is
reading during dinner, an ascetical book and then either
a hagiographical work or something "light". This
amused me to no end when I entered, for I knew that
what Poor Clares call "light reading" would be considered by most persons outside to be very solid stuff. Any
book which does not stand you up in front of your own
soul in a broad daylight that reveals its every dusty crack
and hidden cranny of fault or compromise is called
"light" by the community. However, the books are never
dull. I do not know why anyone should suppose monastic reading would be dull, but I remember that I was
most agreeably surprised as a postulant to discover what
really excellent works were read in the refectory.

Sometimes the reading is momentarily interrupted by
an important announcement from Mother Abbess to the
effect that "The squash is for potatoes. The salad is the
third portion." After years of listening to these quaint
flashes, I still relish them with secret mirth, and not least
because of the judge-like gravity of countenance and
tone with which Mother Abbess unfailingly makes
them.

A Poor Clare dinner consists always of soup, a vegetable, potato, fruit, and the famous "third portion". That last is an ancient monastic term for the main dish of the meal, supposed to be some sort of substitute for the meat we never eat. You are expected to take a substantial helping of "third portion", since Brother Ass must labor on the strength of it until the next day's dinner. Now an innocent-looking salad may be just that, an unimportant sidecar to your vegetable and potato. However, who knows what depths of canned salmon its surface may conceal! Such caches would raise the salad to the rank of a third portion. Consequently, a solemn announcement from the abbess is in order,

Also, the nuns are very set in their monastic ways. If we have no potatoes, then some understudy must be summoned from the culinary wings to play their role. Thus, the pronouncement: "Dear Sisters, the turnips are for potatoes." Now the turnips will most likely be accompanied by cabbage, and the mystery as to which of these two plebs is to rise to potato status is known only to cooks and abbesses, of which I have never been either. But I am unfailingly amused by the revelation, for the implication is that a Poor Clare's digestion would be seriously impaired if she did not know whether cabbage is this day passing itself off as potatoes or preserving the integrity of its name.

The first winter we were in Roswell, we feasted day after day and week after week upon turnips and carrots. It never occurred to anyone to think this monotonous. We had been given turnips and carrots; ergo . . . But their identity was changed from day to day. "Dear Sisters, the carrots are for potatoes", Mother Abbess would solemnly announce on Friday. On Saturday we heard: "Dear Sisters, the carrots are the vegetable; turnips are for potatoes." And on Sunday it got very festive: "Dear Sisters, the carrot salad is the vegetable." When all of us sat on the edge of our chairs on Monday, wondering what variation could possibly remain, Mother Abbess would declaim sweetly and gravely: "Dear Sisters, the carrots and turnips are mixed vegetables and potatoes." Poor Clare abbesses are not easily worsted.

Only the dog objected to all this. It is hard enough on a dog to join a monastic community where there is no hope of a juicy bone because there is never any meat. Scrumptious, our dog, made the best of this, be it said to his credit; but the unvarying carrots and turnips proved too much for either his canine digestion or endurance.

One very mild winter's day, when we had left the door open, Scrum rushed in from the porch, the small saucepan which served him for dinner plate clutched in his white teeth by its handle, and its carrot content untouched. He set the pan down at our feet (we were washing the dishes) and glared at us all with impartial ferocity and no little disgust. Scrum completely disrupted the Rosary which we had been praying, but we got the point.

One of the old nuns had a way, during recreation that winter, of pleasantly reminding one and all of the advantages of carrots for good vision. "Very good for the eyes", she would tirelessly repeat. However, even this impressed Scrumptious not at all. It was obvious that he would have preferred bifocals and a good soupbone. As might be expected, Scrum did not persevere in the monastic life; but no one can deny that he had much to try him.

The nuns return in procession to the choir after dinner, and more prayers are recited for the benefactors of the community. When the dishes are washed and the Rosary recited, all scatter to their private work until the house bell rings out that 2:00 P.M. message of Vespers. This is the great dividing line of the monastic day. If the next day's Office is a major one, it will commence with today's first Vespers. All hearts now turn to a new day. All things are now directed to the coming feast, all becomes a preparation for the next morning's Mass and Holy Communion. The Office of Vespers has, on this account, a singular solemnity. Having labored all the morning, we look now toward evening, singing out with our Lady: "*Magnificat anima mea Dominum*"—"My soul doth magnify the Lord." It is a perfect hour for Vespers. In winter, the day is giving you the fullness of its gray light, as if it, too, magnified the Lord at that hour. In summer, the skies in Roswell are intensely blue, and the sunlight laughs and sings at every window and dances in shimmers on the broad choir floor. "*Magnificat anima mea Dominum!*" it sings. And dust motes turn ecstatically in its beams.

You are given ten minutes to prepare for the glory of Vespers, kneeling quietly in your choir stall and gathering the past morning and early afternoon into the folds of that love you wish to offer God at Vespers. Then, at

2:10, the great Maria bell swings in a deep-throated song: Vespers, Vespers, Evensong. My soul doth magnify the Lord.

10 MORE OF THE SAME

Let the Sisters labor . . . in such a way that, while idleness, the enemy of the soul, is banished, they may not extinguish the spirit of holy prayer to which other temporal things should be subservient.

—RULE OF ST. CLARE

Bells seem to many persons to be a monastic form of tyranny. Before I entered the religious life, a number of acquaintances seized on the bells as the great religious horror. "I could never have my life run by bells." People who shudder delicately at the thought of changing occupation immediately whenever a bell rings are quite unruffled by their own long years of obeying alarm clocks, punching office time-clocks, and rushing to first curtain at the theater.

To a Poor Clare, each bell is the articulation of God's Will. No two bells in a monastic day ring the same message; each is a new summons to a new work for the Lord. Some bells ring always at a specific hour, while others swing out surprises; and to me there is always something adventurous about the bells. Knowing what is said by that little metal tongue of the Lord is like holding the key to a Divine code. If the house bell begins swinging out of season, you may take off your apron on the way down the stairs, for you know that very probably the Archbishop or Father Provincial is in the parlor. A solemn, unscheduled tolling warns you to fly to the infirmary because Sister Death has come to call for one of your Sisters.

It was Saturday in Easter week when Sister Liguori died as matter-of-factly as she had lived. We were scattered at our various Saturday afternoon tasks in the big monastery, with the Vesper alleluias still swimming in our hearts. Everyone was happy-faced with the afterglow of Easter, and no one was worried about Sister Liguori, who was supposed to be in the infirmary for only a brief sojourn after a slight heart attack. A number of the nuns had drifted into the infirmary after dinner and found the patient as cheerful and wittily droll as she usually was. Sister thanked the infirmarian for a good dinner. Her monastic visitors dispersed to their chores and the infirmarian went into the kitchen.

Then Sister Liguori lay back on the pillow, closed her eyes, and died, taking care to drop a metal spoon on the floor to arrest the infirmarian at her work. Precisely as she had lived, without causing distress to anyone, happily, unobtrusively, and thoughtful of others to the very end (the dropped spoon was such a courteous gesture, as all would have been greatly grieved to find her dead body an hour later), she died.

So the infirmarian ran for the abbess, and the house bell began its tolling. Within two minutes, Sister Liguori had all her Sisters around her dying-bed; and within four minutes, Father Leopold had defied all laws of possible human speed to be there, too. And it was her dying-bed and not her deathbed. For, when our good chaplain had quickly anointed her, but hesitated to impart the Papal blessing, Sister Liguori once more, and now for the final time, smoothed out a situation for others. The inert body suddenly gave the slightest of tremors and the smallest of gasps came through the parting lips. "I am alive", thus announced Sister Liguori. "Give me the blessing, and then I will die." So Father blessed her. And she died.

No one wept inconsolably, though everyone loved Sister Liguori. It is only that death is so simple, so familiar—our Sister Death—to Franciscans, that we cannot wail at her visitations. I was present when Mother Abbess was putting a fresh and final guimpe on a dead nun. Mother stepped back and looked down at the peaceful face of her lifeless daughter. "You look very lovely, dear", she said softly and with maternal satisfaction.

Enclosed nuns are not heartless creatures; and for a long time after a Sister's death, her absence whispers sadly in all of our hearts. But under the sadness is a secret, singing joy. Sister Liguori has gone. And we are all coming. We shall not be parted for long.

The bells seem to sense their importance not only when they toll of death, but each time their rigid tongues start wagging. The house bell is earnest and grave about tolling for general work, and solemn for Chapter, but downright roguish about ringing for the

beginning of recreation. It may be a private fancy, but
the bell for the end of recreation always sounds apologetic to me.

If you are out of the monastery, you miss the bells like
the voice of a very intimate friend. I used to keep watch-
ing the clock in the hospital, not to check the time,
but to ring the bells in my mind. Eight-five: Off to the
general work! Eleven-thirty-five: What's on your conscience? Twelve: Maria is pealing out the Angelus; I
wonder what they read in the refectory at dinner? Two:
They are chanting Vespers. You come to feel a vast
loneliness for the bells; and when you are home, it is
sheer luxury to hear them again. Ensconced in our little
cell after my return to the monastery, I heard the great
bell send its message from God through the cloisters and
the courtyards, the laundry and the boiler room, the
chapel and the choir, until each of the walls gave a
reverberating "*Adsum, Domine*"—"Here I am, Lord!"
"Ah!" I breathed softly to myself. And the verse from
the psalm drifted through my heart, as it so often does
when the bells ring: "I come to do thy Will, O my
God." It is not at all the way I fancy you would feel in
responding to a tyrant's summons.

Bells often spell sacrifice, it is true. You want so much
to finish typing this one page, planting this one furrow,
catching up this one seam. But God grows articulate in
the bell. And you leave the page or the furrow or the
seam, not tight-lipped, but with the willingness of one
who loves answering the call of the Beloved. The very
persons who wince at the notion of living by bells are

often the ones who sigh over the difficulty of knowing God's Will. "If I only knew what to do in these circumstances. . . . If I could foresee the future. . . . Can this really be God's Will?" Well, a Poor Clare knows what to do in all the circumstances of all the days. The bells tell her. She does not trouble about foreseeing the future; the bells will tell her what to do and where to go tomorrow and ten years from tomorrow. And what the bells tell her to do is, beyond any flickering shadow of a doubt, God's Will for her.

After the Maria bell has swung out the message of Vespers and the nuns have chanted the beautiful evensong of holy Church, there is a period of spiritual reading and another Cross prayer. These Cross prayers, by which are meant certain prayers recited with the arms extended wide, are beams of prayers set crosswise on many different hours of the monastic day. They intrigue some new postulants, who conceive the idea of praying privately in that position for an hour, and are hauled out the back door of the choir by their long-suffering Mistress and disabused of their fond notions regarding such unorthodox penances. Other new postulants find holding their arms out in prayer not at all a jolly idea. I remember one young spiritual athlete who used gradually to draw her arms together above her head until the palms touched. The next step was to droop the arms into a circle with the hands clasped, in the position of a prize fighter acknowledging applause after knocking out his beefy opponent. This vision, directly in front of me, used to set my shoulders heaving daily. It remains one of the most engaging sights I have yet seen in the monastery.

Once, a young priest visited the monastery. He had two potential postulants, he said. Wonderful girls. Saints (pre-shrunk, apparently). They spent many hours at a time praying with their arms extended. Old Sister Mechtilde squinted through the grate and leaned hard on her cane. "That's the kind that lasts about two weeks here", she volunteered. Father was shaken, but Sister was sound in her pronouncement. Those who indulge in extraordinary penitential feats in the world are almost unfailingly stubbornly attached to them. The normal girl who finds penitential practices penitential, but sweetens them with joy and roofs them under obedience, is the one who will persevere in the cloister with God's grace. When urged to accept postulants "pious" in the sense of having many penitential exercises in their spiritual files, St. Teresa of Avila had a stock answer: Give me intelligence, and I will teach them the piety.

As the brightness of the monastic day begins to dwindle into evening, work again proceeds apace. No one accomplishes so much with her head or her hands as the one who is nourished by much prayer and fortified by silence. Minutes are precious to Poor Clares because they are continually spilling like gold coins out of the hand of God and purchases must be made with them. With these shining coins, one nun feeds her companions and others clothe them; one dispatches warm gratitude to benefactors and another group buys flowers for the altar and food for the monastic table from the shelves of the cloister garden.

In the two periods of work between breakfast and Sext, and between Vespers and evening meditation, habits are made and books are written, vegetables are raised and flowers are cultivated, psalmody is learned and musicianship is schooled, a big monastery is swept and burnished, a chapel kept lovely for the King, vestments made and altar linens sewn. And through all these and so many more occupations, contemplative prayer always whispers and sometimes sings.

St. John of the Cross says something to the effect that one act of pure love is worth more than a hundred years of activity. It is likewise true that love alone ennobles activity, just as prayer nourishes it. Mere activity of itself is quite meaningless in the eyes of God; but the meanest tasks done out of love for Him burst in glory on His vision. Perhaps the silent Sister cook taking the fat brown loaves from the oven, or canning the pickles which will be sold in the city to help defray our expenses, is tipping the scales of the world in its own favor and in God's. Her sweat and her love and her labor pull their weight in the mystery of salvation as surely as the writings of philosophers or the wonder-revealing beakers of the scientists.

We live in such a noisy world that many of us have come to be afraid of silence. We think that if only we do a great deal, it does not much matter what we are. In fact, we seldom stop to investigate what manner of man we are. The hero of the hour is the one who can accomplish the greatest number of things in the shortest possible time. But he makes a sorry monastic hero. It is not what our Lady did which made her the Queen of Heaven and earth, but what she was.

St. Clare is a true mirror of Mary. She built no hospitals, made no political pronouncements, inaugurated no new system of pedagogy, and wrote no books. In the world's eyes, she just did nothing at all. But what was she? Holy Church declares that she was and is a light more shining than light itself. The Church delights to frolic with her name: Clare, light. The Office of her Feast is shot through with the beams of that light which she was. And when the last speech has been made and the last atom shattered, St. Clare will still be a "bright light illuminating all the world".

She was a citadel of silence, and that is why she answers a crying need of our time. We have forgotten how to be silent; we have grown afraid. Yet nothing truly great or enduring was ever yet or will ever be achieved without silence. "While all things were in quiet silence, thy almighty Word, O God, leaped down from Heaven." In the singing silences of eternity that Word was begotten in the bosom of the Father, and the Holy Spirit proceeded as their mutual Love ablaze with silence.

Poor Clares are very busy women. They do not rush madly from one activity to another, because they are more interested in being than in doing. But they accomplish a great deal even on the material side for that very reason. In the rich silence of the monastic life, the energy saved from chatter and clangor flows into prayer and work.

Afternoons in the monastery differ in complexion. Tuesday afternoons are scrubbed and rosy-cheeked washdays, when fragrant clean wash is piled high in the community room, waiting for hands to fold or mend it. Friday afternoons are humble in countenance, as befits hours which embrace the monastic Chapter. Saturday afternoons are bright-eyed and bustling with preparations for Sunday and the expectation of having your sins forgiven in the weekly confession.

The weekly Chapter of faults is one of the most beautiful of monastic usages. St. Gertrude once had a vision wherein she saw the prayers of the nuns at Chapter falling like pearls before the Throne of God. To bow your forehead to the floor and voluntarily accuse yourself of your little public faults and failings of the past week and humbly beg for a penance to atone for them is a privilege so sacred that you must wait a whole year before you can enjoy it. Postulants are not admitted to the Chapter, save when they troop in to hear the announcement of the investiture date of one of their number.

Anyone who thinks it demeaning publicly to admit her faults and to be publicly reproved for them is the one who has never tasted the clean joy of rising up afterward like one refreshed and revivified. No one accuses another at a Poor Clare Chapter. Each novice or nun spontaneously accuses herself. And, indeed, to speak of the faults of another or in any way to call attention to them is considered the gravest of faults in oneself. Mother Abbess alone corrects, for from her alone flows the grace

and streams the light of God by which we are encouraged to overcome the weaknesses of our character and
temperament and to straighten the warped wood of our
judgment. Musicians and artists pay handsome sums to
be corrected by masters for the flaws in their work. Yet,
what is perfection at the console or on canvas compared
to perfection of the soul?

The privilege of being corrected is one of the greatest
privileges of a religious. And the most pitiable religious
in the world is the one whose reaction to correction has
been such that the superior will no longer admonish her.
Religious have a duty binding under pain of mortal sin
to strive for perfection. The abbess' complementary duty
is to correct her nuns "humbly and in charity", as our
holy Mother St. Clare so sweetly and characteristically
expresses it.

Many recommendations are made to the nuns each
week at Chapter for prayers. One that never fails to
touch me is that for "all mothers in the blessed state of
expectancy". Here is another working demonstration of
how truly and how fully the cloistered nun belongs to
the world and the world to her. The whole universe is
her personal charge. It is only fitting that she should
pray, therefore, for the tiny persons being fashioned under the hearts of their mothers and who will shortly be
under her spiritual care. That Poor Clares live by the
hard-headed and warm-hearted practicality of St.
Francis and St. Clare is aptly witnessed by their solicitude for mothers and their unborn babes. Little lives
grow and wax strong in the souls of the contemplative

religious as in the bosoms of their natural mothers. Monsignor Guardini has masterfully depicted the interdependence of the married state and the state of consecrated virginity. He would approve the Poor Clares' weekly prayers at Chapter, where the married state is accorded full appreciation and reverence, and cloistered virgins pray for "all mothers in the *blessed* state of expectancy".

Often the abbess confers with all her nuns at Chapter on matters regarding the spiritual and temporal welfare of the community, remembering the counsel of our holy foundress that "God often reveals to the least that which is best." Thus the community operates always as a spiritual unit in which the opinion of each is considered by all and weighed by the abbess. The afternoons marked with Chapter are especially dear to the community. A more profound silence enfolds the monastery after the Chapter of faults, and work recommences with new stores of spiritual energy.

Saturday afternoon is another monastic institution. Moderns who have "outgrown" Sunday and made it just one more working day are kicking hard against the goad of their own nature. Body and soul were fashioned by God to labor six days and to rest on the seventh, and only when they are permitted to operate according to the Divine specifications do they cooperate in producing contentment. Sunday is so sacred a day in the monastery that each Saturday gets newly excited about it. Sunday is such a great event that the whole schedule of Saturday afternoon is adjusted to prepare for it. Brooms slide, dusters fly, postulants stitch fresh linen bands on their little black veils, the cook makes raisin bread, fresh flowers lift their heads on every altar in summer, and everyone hurries about with the expression of one making last-minute preparations for a signal event. Everyone is. The Lord's day is coming, and it will be the sweet converse of bustling Saturday, the awaited supplement to all the other days.

Ordinary afternoons are never ordinary. They may bring anything from a bushel of over-ripe fruit to whose deck all hands are hastily summoned for a canning session, to an emergency practice of the play to be presented for Archbishop Byrne when he comes to Roswell to officiate on the Feast of our holy Mother St. Clare. Nothing makes a Poor Clare smile as quickly as those good old pious tomes which urge nuns to bear up under the monotony of the cloister and to keep a stiff upper lip in the face of the tedious sameness of monastic living. I have not been able to lay hold on any monotony so far, though I have sighed after it more than once. There seems little to hope for either; for the old nuns looking toward their golden jubilee in the monastery complain that they haven't been able to run down any monotony in the course of fifty years. It is a bit discouraging. For, if contemplatives living their adventurous and ever-changing cloister days and years for God knew where these old masters found their monotony, all the nuns would be fast on its trail.

During our holy Mother St. Clare's seventh centenary year, 1953, we practiced long and hard at rehearsing

Candle in Umbria, the verse-play story of her life. At the same time, the new chapel and wing were under construction. We would rush in from painting and hammering to rehearse the scene where young Clare sings with her sisters and then confides to Agnes her dream of joining St. Francis in his way of life. That was all right. So was the ballet with Lady Poverty. So was the scene of St. Clare's investiture by St. Francis. But then we progressed to the third act, where she confounds the Saracen invaders with the Blessed Sacrament.

The act opens on the community of nuns gathered around the aging and ailing St. Clare. They talk of the barbarous Saracens in fear and trembling. Then Sister Illuminata sees them advancing on the monastery. The script calls for a piercing shriek. It sounds simple, but proved otherwise.

Poor Clares never get much of a chance to keep up on their shrieking. There is very little to scream about in the cloister, and you get so accustomed to the quiet that the loud talk you hear, if you have to leave the cloister for some reason, startles and unnerves you. At the first rehearsal, Sister Colette, who was cast as Illuminata, ran to the makeshift balcony railing right on schedule. She then emitted what even a silent nun could not possibly term a shriek. A broken-down sopranic squeak was all her cloistered lungs could produce.

Such talk as was necessary for direction of the play was permitted, so I was free to expostulate with the squeaking Illuminata. "That will never do", I declared with what sternness I could muster. "Shriek, dear Sister, shriek!—don't peep like an ailing hen." Sister Colette obediently took a deep breath, gave out with another rusty creak and looked at me in hopeless apology. "Here, listen," I said energetically, "listen to me do it." I opened my mouth cavernously, while all the other Poor Clare actresses steeled themselves against the expected piercing scream. My shriek came out like the croupy baby sister of Sister Colette's shriek. "My goodness", I said confusedly. "Maybe you had better go out to the laundry and practice screaming. We've lost the knack of it."

She did. Sunday afternoons found Sister Colette screaming and screaming in the laundry. She finally worked her way up to a really blood-curdling yell. I was immensely pleased. You could see those Saracens, knives in their teeth, when you heard *this* scream. On Monday afternoon, we hurriedly put our paintbrushes to soak in turpentine and rushed into the refectory, which was serving us as auditorium. The bricklayers were hard at their bricklaying in the new dormitory, but we forgot all about them. Sister Colette beheld the invisible advancing horde of Saracens and screamed gorgeously.

Mother Abbess had gone upstairs to see the head of the construction crew. She was on hand to see the men drop their bricks and mortar trowels and go pale. Down below, I was commending Sister Colette. "Better try it again, so you keep the feel of it." Sister obliged with another chilling scream. And another. And yet another. "Wonderful", I beamed. Upstairs, one of the bricklayers stood with fists clenched. "What's goin' on?" A few others pawed the air. One big fellow was apparently going to the rescue, when poor Mother Abbess dragged her stricken voice out of the cement which had formed in her chest during all this. "It's all right", she soothed. "The young nuns are practicing a play." This startled the men no little. "A play?" their faces asked. "What kind of thriller-chillers do cloistered nuns put on, anyhow?" "It's the life of our holy Foundress", added Mother Abbess sweetly. This, I think, left the bricklayers with thoughts too deep for words.

This play, *Candle in Umbria*, came into being as a loving tribute to our Mother St. Clare in her jubilee year, and because Sister M. Eda, S.S.N.D., my friend of many years, had written: "It is so difficult to find suitable plays. I wish you would write one." To our happy surprise, the play was enthusiastically welcomed by high schools and colleges and went into a second printing within six months. We were surprised, because it had begun as a private undertaking which we never dreamed would one day be presented in New Guinea, Ireland, England, and India. We were happy because the play's success proved nothing so much as that the appeal of St. Francis and St. Clare is indeed ageless and overwhelming. We have now amassed a sizeable collection of pictures from *Candle* as performed throughout the country, with little high-school Clares and college Clares, tall and short and dark and blonde Clares. St. Clare must surely love every one of them!

I have been asked about my method of playwriting. And I have been glad at such times that our correspondence is very sharply curtailed, for it would be a great shame to have to write trustful students that I have no method at all! Our plays, like our poems, simply happen. *Counted as Mine*, the three-act play about our Lady's Guadalupan apparitions, was nothing but a prolonged act of love and whisper of tenderness. When I finished scrubbing the bathroom floor, mowing the front lawn, or peeling the turnips, I would sit in our cell just under the six-inch picture of our Lady of Guadalupe; and I would look and look at her. Then I would write another scene.

When our dear Lord later decided He wished me to have some professional training in playwriting technique, He dispatched a superb dramatist and teacher, Dr. Natalie White, from the University of Notre Dame, Indiana, to Roswell, New Mexico. Afterward, reflecting on the strangeness of propounding dramatic structures at a cloister grille, and having learned something of our highly uncomplicated way of living, thinking, and loving, Natalie said she supposed I must have said: "Lord, I need some schooling in drama, but I can't go to the university now." Whereupon the Lord replied: "True enough. Never mind, I'll send the university to you." And Natalie added that she hoped none of us would ever take it into her cloistered head to ask the Lord for the university's golden dome.

As with writing, so with all else. Work is done simply and without consideration for the comparative dignity of varying tasks or enterprises. Such comparisons could never be anything but specious for cloistered nuns, whose work has a common dignity in that it is done with a common love and for one Lover.

Monday, Tuesday, Wednesday, and their hard-working companion afternoons, meet at the same point from which their separate paths departed: the Blessed Sacrament. At 4:45 P.M., the nuns bring the fatigues of the day to the refreshment which is the Lord. "Come to me," He said, "all ye who labor, and I will refresh you." So the day which began in Him and flowed in minutes and hours out of His Heart, now returns to give Him its contented fatigue.

How beautiful a thing work is, that God should promise His own refreshment to it. After a hymn and the Rosary, you disappear into the utter solitude of the evening meditation. You kneel in your stall with all your Sisters around you and your Lord on His throne before you. And you are completely alone in the company you love best on earth. At 5:30 you emerge from the depths of your solitude and affirm your refreshment with another hymn.

Again the monastic procession forms to the soul-stirring measures of the *Miserere mei, Deus*, and comes into the summer-sunlight or winter-twilight of the refectory for collation. Before that simple repast is taken, another very beautiful monastic usage finds its place. All the nuns fall to their knees and prostrate on the floor, each to beg pardon of all the others for anything she may have done during the day to give pain or mortification to her Sisters. Each nun begs her companions to pray that she may receive our Lord more worthily the next morning in Holy Communion for His greater honor and her own salvation and perfection. The abbess then recommends the intentions of our civil and spiritual superiors and of all those by whom the community's prayers have been asked that day. It is a cleansing and transforming little ceremony. We rise up feeling washed and forgiven, ready to begin again.

There is free time after collation for the Stations of the Cross, for an informal visit to the Lord Jesus, or what you will. And then, at 6:30, there is recreation. Recreation is hard on the roof, but wonderful for all those under it. I remember feeling warmly happy when one retreat master, an aged and experienced friar, declared that the unfailing gauge of a community's fervor is the hilarity of its recreations. All's well, I thought, all's well.

Prospective postulants often inquire about what we do at recreation. Read? Play games? No? Well, what do we do? We talk. Reading at recreation is forbidden. Games exist in the form of a standing joke. Entertainment is strictly on the home front, and never wanting. Silence alone fits us to speak. It alone conditions us for the joy of sometimes talking. The old cartoons showing the despairing hostess when the radio or television set breaks down and there is "nothing to do" move us not to mirth but to pity. Conversation, which started out to be an art and a tremendous God-given privilege, is well on the way to becoming a lost art today and little esteemed as an inheritance from the Divine Word. Except in cloisters. Only the silent know how to talk, and that is why we cannot imagine anything more delightful to do at recreation than just to talk. Chesterton thanked God for being so ingenious as to "fill our stockings with our legs". Poor Clares thrill to His having been so inventive as to place tongues in our mouths, for having given them the power to communicate ideas and share insights, to jest and to laugh. They thank God for the power and guard it preciously through silent hours.

The wonderful hour over, the community returns to the choir for Compline. "Into Thy hands, O Lord, I commend my spirit", chant the postulants in eager young voices. "Into Thy hands", sing out the superiors, who place all the burdens of office in those Divine hands. "I commend my spirit", the old nuns tremulously chant. And each nun rehearses the moment when Sister Death will come to take her own hand: "Now, O Lord, thou dost dismiss thy servant . . . for my eyes have seen thy salvation." It was of this I thought when the poem "Parousia" took shape in my heart.

> I have set a candle in each window of my soul,
> I hold the thousand bellropes of my heart
> Against the sign . . .
> Against the possible sudden splendor of—
> Tonight!

Compline is more than the perfect night prayer. It is an immediate preparation for death, which is always the possible splendor of each night.

The lights are lowered. The great silence takes the monastery into its velvet arms. Each nun enters the private castle which is her little cell and kisses the floor of it. "The Heart of Jesus is the place of my rest", she says. The day is ended. Her lamp is trimmed for the midnight summons of the Bridegroom.

11 IN ALL THINGS, ONE

And if a mother love and nurture her daughter according to the flesh, how much the more ought a Sister to love and nurture her Sister according to the Spirit.

—RULE OF ST. CLARE

I had not made the acquaintance of Blessed Giles, confessor of the First Order, before I entered the monastery. This was my misfortune. For, anyone who has lived for twenty years without knowing Brother Giles has missed a great deal. His vocation to the Franciscan Order, like everything else in his life, was as uncomplicated as the man himself, for Giles of Assisi was a man of clear vision. He looked at the young Francis of Assisi and his community of friars (to the number of two, Bernard Quintavalle and Peter Catani), and he looked longer at what they were doing. He found no discrepancy between what Francis, Bernard, and Peter were preaching and what they were doing; and he liked both. So he went to St. Francis, fell on his knees, and asked to be accepted into the tiny fraternity. He became the famous Brother Giles and retained his wondrous insight to the end of his days.

Brother Giles was not a product of the schools, but a peasant. He was not versed in the sciences or trained in the polished turning of a phrase. Yet, his native wit was always delicious and sometimes devastating. And he could be scathing on occasion, when his sense of humility was offended. A pious soul who declared that in a vision of hell no Franciscan was ever seen may or may not have piously fainted (it is not recorded) at Giles' retort: "You did not look deep enough." But Brother Giles could also be as tender as a woman. His method of explaining and defending the perpetual virginity of the Mother of God was to strike the ground once: a virgin before the birth of Christ!—and summon a miraculous lily into bloom. A virgin at His birth!—and, behold! a second lily. A virgin after His birth and forever!—and a third lily springs up to witness his word.

As we might expect from all this, when Brother Giles spoke of the common life, his words were few as they always were and as heavily freighted with meaning as any ever were. He had a right to speak of fraternal charity, because he practiced it all through the painful years when he stood loyally by his beloved Father Francis and watched the golden edges of the Franciscan ideal being persistently gnawed by some of the brethren. His life was a long, clear echo of Francis' life, continuing to resound after the saint's death as both warning and recall. Yet, when Brother Giles did speak of charity, it was in phrases so short and limpid that it needs something of his own wisdom and love to comprehend them for the marvelous synthesis of the common life which they actually are.

"The greatest grace that a man can have under Heaven is to know how to live well with those among whom he dwells." There is, in that simple declaration, an eternity of meaning. Small wonder that St. Francis so esteemed his "firebrand Giles". Not surprising that St. Clare loved and admired Giles so much. His simple wisdom was too chaste and terrible for sophistries.

To Brother Giles, truth was the food of the strong, and he liked it served up plain. What he thoroughly disliked was disguising its flavor with the condiments of many words. Once, when St. Clare had invited a celebrated preaching friar from foreign parts to address her nuns, Brother Giles accompanied him. Giles suffered the preaching a while, and then took over the situation as only Giles could. "Sit down, brother, for you have talked long enough. Now I will speak to them." And Brother Giles spoke, like cleansing flames. Such a man would not have styled the worthy living of the common life "the greatest grace that a man can have under Heaven" merely to be sententious. He spoke as a member of the First Order of St. Francis. If God had elected to create Giles female and call him to the enclosed Second Order, Sister Giles could have underlined her words in gold.

No one who has not lived in a cloister can fully understand just how intertwined are the lives of cloistered nuns. Their hearts may be wide as the universe and bottomless as eternity, but the practical details of their living are boxed up into the small area within the enclosure walls. Cloistered nuns rub souls as well as elbows all their lives, and if they do not step out of themselves to get a true perspective on themselves and on others, they can become small-souled and petty and remain immature children all their lives long.

A vocation to the enclosed contemplative life is a rare vocation. What stronger bonds could we have than our common vocation, our common ideals, our common Love? None. And we live so very closely, how could there be a possibility of those frequent and painful misunderstandings which cause so much suffering among persons in the world? The fact is, we understand one another all too well.

When I was in the novitiate, a postulant once remarked brightly at recreation that it surprised her how quickly she had come to know the others so well. "It takes a long time really to get to know someone outside," Nancy said, "but not here." Sister Catherine's black eyes shot out sparks of impish merriment. "Nancy, after you've been here for six weeks, we know you better than your mother ever did!" Nancy first gasped, and then laughed with the rest of us. It is so true.

Poor Clares know their fellow nuns down to the fingerprints. We see one another's faults in the shadowless daylight of the cloister. We are too close to miss a fleeting expression. (No distractions!) We sense moods and vibrate to overtones of words. (It's so quiet, don't you know!) And it is the business of each individual nun to decide whether she will let this unique meshing of lives and hours make her a compassionate woman with a vast and tender pity for the weaknesses of her Sisters, as well as a solid admiration for their striving, or let it keep her a perpetual spiritual adolescent in a continual state of shock over the faults of others and occupied in dressing the wounds of her own afflicted vanity and sensibilities.

That wonderful woman, St. Teresa of Avila, used to say in that cryptic way of hers: "Nothing ever shocks me." She added that the true proof of charity is never to be shocked, but only to redouble our efforts to practice the virtue opposed to the fault we have seen. The shock-squadrons in religious life are invariably composed of those who do not know the abc's of their own souls, for the best way to lull yourself into a stupor regarding your personal failings is to keep a weather eye trained on the defects of others. That is why eyebrow-hoisting is a sport not encouraged in monasteries.

A Trappist monk once wrote to me: "When you are convinced that there is no fault or sin, no matter how terrible, of which you are not capable, you will just have begun to understand humility." Our holy Mother St. Clare cautions her daughters almost airily "not to be worried or angry over the fault of anyone". She was a great woman, mature enough to draw a conclusion like this: "For anger and worry hinder charity in themselves as well as in others." She would like her nuns to remember the monk of the towering rages. He died in one such moment, having burst a vein in his head; and his abbot feared the monk was lost. Did he not die in his sin of anger? No religious suffrages for such a one! So the patient Lord had to send the dead monk's spirit back to earth to teach the abbot better. "I died not of my rage but from the effort of overcoming it." And, touching his halo respectfully to his superior, the monk returned to bliss.

If we can judge so wrongly of something great, what snares the little failings of others can set for our poor judgment! That is why God does not recommend judging. In fact, it is rather a sore point with Him, His business, which He delegates to no one.

The fact that cloistered nuns love one another with all their hearts, and that there is no one in the community who would not cheerfully die for any or all of the others, does not mean that Sister Paula's slow and ponderous ways do not cause internal combustion in quick little Sister Celeste, who works with her. It does not imply that keen-witted Sister Teresa will not be scorched by the small flames of impatience that stolid Sister Agnes' ways so often kindle for her. Sister Helen is naturally timid, and letting others manage affairs is sheer bliss to her; but Sister Anne is a born leader and takes charge of any situation as naturally as breathing. One is quick-tempered. Another plods. One leans toward vanity and another tilts toward being slovenly. The perfectionists justify their views by the avowal that nothing can ever be good enough for God. The phlegmatics just as truly reflect that God wants only our perfection and not the perfection of our works. So it goes. Each one is right. And everyone can be wrong.

The common life is, therefore, the mortification supreme. By nature, we all like the sound of trumpets and the sight of a heraldic blaze, at least in our own hearts, when we suffer. Night-long vigils, black fasts, extra disciplines all smack of sanctity to the immature. Merely to trudge along, lost in the ranks of cabbage and boiled-potato dinners, on broom-and-duster detail, with routine penances coming up on schedule, seems a mean road to Heaven. It is. And precisely there is its glory.

Women, even the most stolid of them, have some sort of originality in their very bloodstream. If Mrs. Van Plume discovers Mrs. Absynthe-Jones in a gown like her own newest one, Mrs. V. P.'s afternoon is ruined. The gown is ready for the mission barrel as far as she is concerned. Now, Poor Clares haven't a ghost of a chance to be stunning by their singularity; the founders saw to that. They also took pains to spare Poor Clares of the future, as well as those then present, the need of taking time for embellishments. We have no shoes to shine, no leather girdles to keep spruce, no pleats to press, no starched guimpes or ruffs to maintain. The utter simplicity of our habit and headdress came home to my mind as well as my heart when Pope Pius XII began issuing recommendations about simplifying and modernizing Sisters' garb.

We belong to one of the oldest Orders in the Church, yet our ancient dress is so modern and uncomplicated that we can perform feats quite beyond the reach of many of the newest Congregations. We do not practice broad jumps, but we could if required. We can eat corn on the cob with the greatest of ease. Our unstarched guimpes and soft, flat veils care not a fig for the wilting properties of Sister Rain. We could see traffic on the left and the right, if there were any traffic handy.

As with every other aspect of the common life, the common dress brings glad compensations as well as mortification. And it does remain one of God's prettiest minor miracles that Nancy, whose glittering wardrobe enriched a dozen of her girlfriends when she entered the cloister, is now oblivious of the fact that the black tape around her garden cape has become an off-emerald shade under the New Mexico sun.

This sun-fade had us blinking in more ways than one when we came to Roswell. We discovered that, unless we wanted to invest in a new serge habit once a year, we had better not wear serge in the garden. So Mother Abbess bought some gray rayon for garden habits. Beautiful stuff, we approved. Just the color of our good habits. It was indeed, until it was washed. After that, the gardeners wielded their hoes with pink-sleeved arms. "No more of that!" Mother Abbess ex-cathedrated. "We'll save that for Third Order shrouds." This seemed like a capital idea, as the departed members of the Third Order in Roswell and environs would scarcely have laundry worries.

Mother then invested in some guaranteed-not-to-fade we'll-pay-you-back-otherwise denim. The new novices looked fresh and sweet in it. The stuff emerged from the washing machine retaining its identity. But the Roswell sun did not care for the shade. It bleached the new habits nearly white. "We'll dye 'em", we said grimly. "We have to look alike, cost what it may." Dye we did. And nearly die we also did when the different fabrics drank in the dye with decidedly varying effects. Sister Paula roamed the little orchard in chocolate brown. Sister Anne cooked in an exciting rustshade garment. Sister Catherine's habit leaned toward burnt orange. We called ourselves the Rainbow Girls, and decided to try no more.

The queen unsurpassed in this great color epoch, as far as I am concerned, remains our dear Mother Vicaress. The back of her habit was well worn (which is a Poor Clare euphemism for a sort of decomposition resulting from extreme old age), so she attached a new serge rear section to the good advance guard. The old serge in front, however, was so faded by this time that the repairs produced a ravishing two-tone effect that no Parisian designer would have dared to sponsor even for her most extreme clients. Mother Vicaress advanced toward you in pinkish brown and retreated in quiet gray, and always with that dignity peculiar to herself.

There was a time when I took it a bit hard that our hues were so un-akin. Now I notice it only when I see a new postulant's eyes flicking over the sorry uncommonness of our common dress. Little Postulant Eleanor knew she should not talk to professed Sisters, but she could not resist the fascination of Sister Catherine's burnt orange garden habit. "Are you an Oblate?" she wanted to know. It reminded me of the long conferences I had with myself when I was a new postulant and beheld Sister Emmanuel sailing about in a black habit. It was the only one on the premises, so I conjectured that Sister Emmanuel must be doing public penance. I burned to know for what, as Sister Emmanuel had the face and bearing of an unusually recollected angel, the type of angel whom I felt the Lord could hold up as an example to young and boisterous cherubim. "You can't go by faces, I guess", I told myself. It turned out later that a former abbess had bought some new gray material for night habits and, in the trusting manner of nuns, never unpacked it until the need was at hand. Black it was, a fine, sooty, unequivocal black. Nothing to do by then but use the stuff. And because Sister Emmanuel was cook at the time, she wore her black night habit in the heat of the kitchen instead of her serge habit. My apostate angel proved to be merely an angel.

So, too, the differences which most high poverty necessitates in the common dress prove to be the splendor of its uniformity. Our holy Father St. Francis and our Mother St. Clare were too great of soul to trouble themselves unduly over fading hues or about a poor little piece of denim trying valiantly and failing ignominiously to look like serge with the help of ten cents' worth of dye. I look a bit enviously at Sister Colette's sickly-gray garden habit with the reinforced elbows, because I think it would be St. Clare's selection if she came to look over our wardrobe.

St. Clare legislated that the abbess and vicaress are to conform to the common life in all things. So, how much more the others! St. Clare's idea of the prerogatives of a superior was entirely novel in her century. A Poor Clare abbess boasts neither staff nor train. She wears no pectoral cross, but the same little wedding ring ($2.50 net) as her daughters. Our abbess is currently resplendent in a large patch across the front of her habit. It was put there by her own hands, the same hands that quarter and deworm apples with the best of them, the same hands that wield a dish towel like a professional.

St. John Berchmans had a stock answer for anyone who asked him what he found most difficult in religion. "The common life", he admitted. That is where enclosed contemplatives have the edge on all other religious. They have no escape into outside work, and can never blow a farewell kiss to their Sisters and be off to the ward or the classroom or the day nursery. Neither have they the luxury of eremitical solitude. They live alone in very close company. And if they do that well, they have "the greatest grace a man can have under Heaven".

Many persons who stand up well enough alone make a poor showing in company. It is far easier for a woman to work herself weary under the steam of her own initiative than to fall gladly into someone else's broom-and-bucket brigade. So, if you want to scent out a potential Poor Clare saint, do not pause overlong at the nun who accomplishes great laborious feats single-handed, but look for the one who is big enough to do things some other nun's way. Just to let herself be lost in an ever-unscattering crowd can be a woman's martyrdom.

Women were created by God to be mistresses of their households. There are in the monastery at Roswell today, therefore, sixteen potential mistresses of households, fifteen of whom will always and at any given moment remain potential. "Use your initiative", our Lord urged the Poor Clare mystic in the monastery at Jerusalem,

Sister Mary of the Trinity, "in leaving to others the pleasure of commanding." The Lord, He is wise! It demands the very fullest use of a woman's initiative to efface herself in the details of work as of so many other things.

The uncommon mortification of the common life is felt again in the time for doing things. You have just put full steam ahead on your window-washing when the bell rings for chant practice. So you go to chant practice, where one may get the rhythm false and another may blast on the high notes. Or, you feel very reflective this evening and want so much to be alone with your thoughts. But it is time for recreation. And Sister Catherine is in her most hilarious mood. If you understand this uncommon common life, you will shake off your pensiveness as thoroughly as a puppy shakes off the drops of cool water after his swim and match Sister Catherine quip for quip. If you are virtuous enough, perhaps you will outclass her!

In moments of intense personal suffering, even the small clatter of common living can be magnified by raw nerves into an almost insupportable burden. St. Thérèse used to set her jaw against the rosary-rattling nun behind her in the choir. Any cloistered nun understands precisely what the Little wrought-iron Flower felt.

One of God's most profound secrets is the mystery of suffering. Our founders knew this when they set down in our Constitutions: "For one may be more enfeebled by a passing indisposition than another by a grave and prolonged illness." The nun who gives an impatient answer in the evening may be the one whose soul is shining with the splendor of the unnoticed patience she has practiced all day with a raging headache. A show of wounded feelings may indicate nothing less than a valiant heart reaching the final outpost in a desert of desolation.

So, too, there is no scale for balancing the apparent virtues of one nun against those of another. The negligible act of humility which costs one character nothing may be an act of genuine heroism in some other. Chesterton regarded the cold statue of the saint and wondered: "Who knows the secret tears at night, the scourges of regret?" And Gertrude von Le Fort wisely observed that we love one another across an abyss. Occasionally in the cloister one nun may unexpectedly gain a new insight into the character or temperament or secret pain of another. Such moments have come to me, and I have been shaken and stirred profoundly by the unmasking. And I have been confirmed in my respect for the unpretentious valor of those with whom I live and whose nobility so often passes unnoticed. Even in minor matters, none of us is equipped, much less authorized, to pronounce on the merits of our companions. It is not likely that the Franciscan martyrology of the twenty-first century will mention that Sister Celeste forswore taking slow and deliberative Sister Paula firmly by the shoulders with orders to "Move along! Move along!" in the Poor Clare laundry in Roswell, New Mexico, and thus consummated her martyrdom. No more will it mention the touching death of Sister Helen, whose sensitive ears had been deafened by the clangors of a few monastic racers during the general work. Very probably, no eulogium will be found there of Sister Teresa, who heroically bit her tongue in three pieces so as not to suggest a more efficient way for others to do their work. But who knows what books God keeps, Who created that enigmatic creature, woman!

The aged abbess in Chicago was fond of reminding her nuns that many patient lambkins fit in a very small stable. Many unruly, long-horned sheep do not. Courtesy pretends to be the virtue of the gentle and retiring. Actually, it is the hallmark of the strong. A Poor Clare in a small cloistered monastery finds this out in short order. A courteous compliance to an unreasonable request when she is overburdened with other duties, a courteous ear for those who bore her, a courteous face for the officious who chafe her, are the identifying marks of one whom St. Clare can recognize at a glance as her own daughter.

In his Bull of her canonization, Pope Alexander IV wrote of our holy Mother St. Clare: "The perfect order of her charity, the sweetness of her love, the strength of her patience, the peace which united hearts, all were found united in the soul of this virgin. She was soft-spoken, gentle of manner, and to God and man she was most lovable and precious." These are the words of a strong man of God about a strong woman of God. They are more than memorable. They form an appendix to the common life which St. Clare so valued and which she so faithfully followed. Her Rule is studded with the recurring phrase "And the abbess shall do likewise." She knew so well that the measure of a religious is her ability to "do likewise". And she did not intend to cheat the abbess of this glory.

God seems to exercise His Divine humor when He peoples cloistered monasteries. Apparently, He casts a Divine glance over the entire nation to select with infinite care the score or so of young women who are most unlike in every possible respect. When His summoning grace has brushed against the hearts of fiery Latins and stolid Germans, high-strung musicians and sanguine high-school girls, teachers of vast enthusiasms and timid clerks, the Lord seems to feel He has the nucleus of a normal community of cloistered nuns! That a selection like this can grow into a group of consecrated women who love one another to such an extent that they can spend forty or fifty years in the closest kind of living, accepting each other's foibles of character and temperament with patience and compassion, is part of the mystery of God's wisdom and His love.

One of our good benefactors in Roswell had a sharp insight into the common life and a homely way of expressing it. When a group of other secular friends was discussing the penitential practices of the newly arrived Poor Clares, this shrewd lady terminated the seminar with the flat observation: "Penances, nothing! If they didn't do anything but stay cooped up in there all their lives, that would be enough." This pithy resolution was relayed to us. We smiled.

"Cooped up" we are. We never put on our hats and go for a walk. But we run down the avenues of God's love. "Behold, how they love one another!" pagans marveled at the early Christians. It is the particular marvel of cloisters. Any cloister at which men could not so marvel is already in ruins, however tall its enclosure wall, however imposing its towers.

12 WILD AND SWEET

The form of the life of the Order of the Poor Sisters, which the blessed Francis founded, is this: to observe the holy Gospel of our Lord Jesus Christ.

—RULE OF ST. CLARE

"Wild and sweet" was the comment of a Trappist friend who read the Rule of our holy Mother St. Clare for the first time. And it is true that St. Francis and St. Clare would have driven St. Ignatius Loyola mad if they had been appointed to help him write his spiritual exercises! Saint differeth from saint in glory.

"The form of life of the Order of the Poor Sisters, which the Blessed Francis founded, is this: to observe the holy Gospel of our Lord Jesus Christ." When we read these opening words of the first chapter in the Rule, we may ask: "Is that all?" Where other Orders have many prescriptions as wise as they are workable, the Order of St. Clare has almost none. Just to observe the holy Gospel sounds like a comfortable enough business. Yet even Francis and Clare did not find it so, however giant their sanctity. Our holy Mother St. Clare practiced the faith and the poverty laid down in the Gospel at the

cost of a whole lifetime of suffering. Her faith moved
the mountain of the Papacy only two days before her
death, and her worn hands that had pleaded for the
poverty of the Gospel had the cold sweat of her death
agony on them when the approved Rule of "most high
poverty" was placed in them.

The Rule of St. Clare is so demanding precisely because it is so simple. What she and St. Francis desired
solely was the closest possible union with God by the
closest possible imitation of the God-Man. Nothing,
then, could be more logical than to take His Gospel as
their form of life. Christ said that He is the Way, and
Francis and Clare meant to follow Him quite literally. "I
am the Life", He declared, so Francis and Clare set out
to live Him. They believed everything Christ said because He is the truth, and they were incapable of those
glosses at which lesser souls are so adept. How well they
succeeded is testified by history. Our holy Father St.
Francis was called "the Christ of Umbria". And St. Clare
was as Francis' second soul.

Chesterton withered the poet who disdained the "lilies and languors of virtue" for the "roses and raptures of
vice" with a smile. "If you think virtue is languor," the
big man with the Franciscan heart rejoined, "just try it,
and see!" When the Trappist monk admired our holy
Rule as wild and sweet, he cut to the core of it. It is wild
because it demands a wholesale divesting of one's self,
not just a doffing of the outer mantle. It is sweet in the
rewarding peace and deep, singing joy of such a divesting. To those who think that the time has now come to

be up and doing in an entirely active way, and who consider that the Rule of St. Clare is merely the impractical dream of a romantic medieval woman, we smile: "Just try it, and see." For the others, who bewail our impossibly hard lot and declare that the primitive Rule demands penance and sacrifice beyond the strength of a woman, we laugh out of the depths of our contentment: "Just try it, and see." Of course, none of these extremists ever does.

It is said that our holy Father Francis never opened his mouth without quoting the Gospel. Actually, he was not so much quoting the words of Scripture as speaking spontaneously out of his own eloquent heart. St. Francis had simply plunged his whole being into the Gospel. His life had merged into the life of Christ. He could not quote, for he had reached that perfect fusion with the mind of our Lord where a tongue extemporizes on the eternal truths in a soul.

The same was true of his daughter, Clare. They accepted the Gospel in such utter simplicity and love that their simplicity loosed all the sophistic knots in the society of their time. When bishops and, later, popes were to object that the way of life St. Francis and St. Clare proposed to their followers was superhuman, impractical, and improvident, our holy Father Francis would turn those searching dark eyes of his upon the objectors with the plea: "I wish only to observe the holy Gospel of our Lord Jesus Christ." Nobody had an answer for that. They could scarcely accuse our Divine Savior of being rash and impractical, though surely all our small human minds would have settled for a less painful way of redeeming than the one God chose.

St. Francis had another rejoinder, too. His daughter, Clare, and her nuns were heroically and joyously living a refutation to the arguments of those who condemned the Franciscan way of the Gospel. Men could not honestly say that the life which frail women, most of them born and reared in softness and luxury, were living so successfully and the ideal they were embracing so warmly were beyond the powers of strong men! After Francis died, Clare had twenty-seven years of life left to her. Through them all, she clung tenaciously to her holy Father's ideal. When the Supreme Pontiff, Gregory IX, who urged her so repeatedly to accept revenues and a stable income, offered to dispense her from her vow of utter Franciscan poverty, St. Clare replied simply, and not without a fine humor: "Holy Father, absolve me from my sins, but not from my vow."

She triumphed only on her deathbed, but that was enough. And when her pure soul escaped her tired body and went to rejoin the soul of St. Francis before the Face of God, St. Clare could well have paraphrased the words of St. Paul and said: "Blessed Father, I have fought a good fight, I have kept our Gospel way, I have finished the course you began."

All that charmed me in my first months in the monastery had strong roots in the Gospel. The childlike love the nuns showed the abbess, and the simple trust the novices reposed in their Mistress, flowered out of the Gospel. The Poor Clares do not promise obedience to their superiors in the manner of the pharisees who said: "The gift!"—politely regretting that their love of God is too utter for sharing. "Your superior needs to feel herself loved", our Lord said to Sister Mary of the Trinity, the Poor Clare in Jerusalem. This is a far cry from the tight-lipped pseudo-sanctity of some spiritual authors. It is an affirmation of St. Clare's dying words.

In her profoundly moving Testament, our Foundress calmly urges her daughters to love: (1) herself; (2) their own souls; (3) the other Sisters. A bit shocking to find the holy Foundress placing herself before the souls of her daughters? No, it is only another instance of her wisdom, which is too terribly simple for the taste of most. Poor Clares who love their Mother St. Clare as they should will also love their own souls as they should. If their love for St. Clare and her way of life falters, at that same moment their love for their own souls becomes faulty and questionable. And then there is no possibility of a genuine fraternal charity, since no one can love another richly and warmly if she does not love her own soul aright.

Each abbess who has succeeded St. Clare down seven arches of centuries takes our Franciscan observance of the holy Gospel into her hands. She must keep the first flame burning and preserve evangelical simplicity in her monastery with jealous guardianship. That is why her admonitions and corrections will always be as direct and uncomplicated as our holy Rule and our blessed Founders. "Be Christlike", Mother Abbess so often urges, knowing how, saying that, she says all for her daughters. I remember hearing her say, when I was a novice: "In any situation, do what you feel sure Christ would do; and you will never go wrong." I have heard her say that a hundred times since, and the counsel remains as wise and as fresh as the Gospel. It is not so difficult to penetrate the mind of Christ, insofar as our imitation of Him is concerned, as we might sometimes like to believe. His Gospel provides us with a practical handbook on daily conduct quite disconcerting to the spurious logic of our fallen human nature, both in its comprehensiveness and in its attention to detail!

Harshness is the thing farthest removed from the Rule of St. Clare, for she wrote as she lived—by the Gospel. Was the gentle Christ ever harsh? When little postulant Eleanor has hoed a hard row in the garden and seeks out her Mistress at 3:30 P.M. with the simple and tragic statement: "Dear Mistress, I'm starving", Eleanor will get something to eat or drink. Because she loved the Christ Who had compassion on the multitude and would not send them away hungry lest they faint in the way, St. Clare wrote in her Rule concerning the fast: "The abbess may charitably dispense as regards the young and the weak." A young friar once awakened St. Francis in the night with the same cry: "I'm starving!" And the blessed Father rose and prepared food and ate with the weak one. He gave the young friar food out of time because he was a prudent superior. He ate with him because he was a loving father. Love alone can inspire us to such delicacy as that. It is the love of the God-Man Who condescended to eat with His disciples even after

His Resurrection, and Who let mean-souled men call Him "a glutton and a drinker of wine".

However real the material poverty in a new foundation like ours, its mortifications only draw us closer to the poor Man of the Gospel, Who sometimes had not whereon to lay His sacred head. The absolute trust in God our Father which the Gospel urges gives us that utter contentment with what we have. We know that God sends us what we need, and thus we can never need anything but what He sends.

Our first winter in Roswell let us taste that contentment to the full. It was a season of record cold; and when we came into the refectory each morning, saluting our Lady with "*Ave, Maria*" through chattering teeth, we found the walls glowing with ice. When the refectorian poured hot coffee into Sister Leonarda's five-cent china cup, the frozen cup protested into shards. So we thanked God that we had an extra cup and that someone had donated coffee, and we admired the sheen of the ice on the walls, while old Sister Leonarda ejaculated: "Well, dear me!", which is one of her very strongest expressions, employed only in moments of crisis or shock.

At the night Office, we wriggled our blue toes in our sandals; and we had recreation on the narrow dormitory stairs (two to a step, for warmth!) because we could not afford to heat the big community room each evening. And we laughed. Christ said we should deny ourselves and take up our cross, and we rejoiced to have this new way to do it. Now there is a heater in the refectory, and the new choir is warm at the night Office. And our happiness retains its status quo, because God is our Father in Heaven, and we like whatever He chooses to provide for us.

Soviet Communists are bitter, cruel men because they force a false common ownership on men. Poor Clares are joyous women because they freely accept no ownership at all, in imitation of the Christ of the Gospel, Who was born in another man's stable and buried in a borrowed sepulchre. What the Soviets breed is hatred and greed. What Franciscans have is love and generosity. I had very real evidence only yesterday afternoon of how practically the abbess as well as the other nuns live by the words of the holy Rule on poverty. "The Sisters shall not appropriate anything to themselves, neither a house nor a place nor anything . . . [but be] as strangers and pilgrims in this world, serving the Lord in poverty and humility", legislates St. Clare, if one can call so lyric an appeal a legislation. Yesterday, I had taken a new suffrage book from the library for our abbess, who needed it. Mother Abbess herself compiled that book and had it published. She is the abbess of the community, and all materialities are in her keeping. But when she stopped me outside the library, she was beaming. "May God reward you for giving me the new book", she said. I could offer only the simple rejoinder: "You're welcome, Mother." This was no pious pretense. It was only the words of our holy Rule living and speaking. A pilgrim is grateful for whatever she is given, even if she happens to be the abbess of the monastery and superior of the librarian.

The evangelical joy of having so little to complicate

our lives lends us all a marked ingenuity for converting sundry articles into highly unorthodox uses. Poor Clares can find a use for anything they are given, we always stoutly maintained; but we thought we had met our Waterloo when a devoted benefactor included a box of Blue Jay corn-and-bunion pads in her donation. Barefoot nuns are spared such trials as require corn-and-bunion pads for their surcease, but ingenious Sister Catherine seized upon the package avidly. The refectory chairs have tiny metal knobs on the bottoms of their legs, and those knobs make little black comments on the bare wood floor, to Sister Catherine's acute distress. After all, a refectorian likes her floor as free of hieroglyphics as the next one. So Sister captured the bunion pads and slapped them energetically onto the feet of the chairs. We could not afford to buy padded glides for the chairs, but they now glide beautifully on Blue Jay bunion pads.

There is a humor about life in general that comes from simple Gospel living. And once we really immerse ourselves in the Gospel, we catch overtones of our Lord's own humor hitherto unsuspected. For example, there is that instance of Christ at Jacob's well. It takes only a very little reflection to open our hearts to a warm companionship with the weary and thirsty Lord leaning against the well, but do we see Him almost *teasing* the profligate Samaritan woman into becoming a prophetess? Only a little more meditation would make us very sure of His joy when that shameless adulteress shook off her sins like greasy drops of stagnant water and ran through the city, calling out: "Is not this the Christ?"

I see our Lord at that moment looking out over those fields white for the harvest, and I know there was a half-smile on His lips and that His dark eyes were dreaming with vision. All the lectures that much-"wed" Samaritan lady had endured had left her quite unmoved. Perhaps they had even irritated her into her alliance with number six. Suddenly, here was this tired young Rabbi Who did not draw His garments closer about Him to spare His person the possible contamination of a brush of robes against hers. This thirsty Stranger was evidently a Man of refinement, yet He only congratulated her on the cunning of her honesty in saying that she had no husband. She had forsaken the legitimate encumbrance of husbands for the terrible fetters of adultery. Christ knew it. And she knew that He knew it. So she capitulated. She gave up adultery for prophecy.

I have always delighted in the mysterious and divine humor of the Almighty Who commissioned the princely Isaiah to proclaim His human coming in glorious poetry, Who spilled whole choirs of angels into the midnight skies over Bethlehem to sing His arrival, Who elected the austere John the Baptist to clear a path for His ministry, and then chose a sinful woman for the climax of it all! "Is not this the Christ?" All the Samaritan's woman's forgotten dignity came alive under His gaze. All her forfeited nobility was redeemed by His compassion. She became a living torch in the city, setting the dry wood of men's hearts on fire with the burning humility of her witness. God wished that no class of human beings should go without its prophet.

If anyone asks: "What has that to do with the Rule of St. Clare?" I answer: "Everything." Dozens upon dozens of Gospel scenes could be recalled here as being bone and lineaments of that Rule which is simply: "To observe the holy Gospel of our Lord Jesus Christ". When strangers come to whisper their tattered little tragedies to the portress or to the abbess, they will find the compassionate ear of those who live by the principles of Christ at Jacob's well. When poor sinners whom the world would call derelicts send us pathetic penciled notes wrapped around a crumpled dollar, they have the shrewd wisdom and the same desperate courage which brought a prostitute to Christ's feet and sent a little Jewish embezzler scrambling up into a sycamore tree to catch a glimpse of His face.

The freedom with which the most tormented and outcast of men and women unburden their souls to cloistered nuns struck me with immense force in the beginning of my monastic life. Mother Abbess would calmly recommend to our prayers and sacrifices the cause of sodden drunkards and sinful women who had scribbled letters to us who are pledged to a lifetime of self-abnegation and whose virginity is perpetually consecrated to God by vow. The rightness of this still moves me profoundly, and it always will. These poor derelicts have a truly practical and instinctive knowledge about the enclosed contemplative life.

At the last outpost of misery, spurned by polite society, these poor sinners know where their final refuge lies. If they listened to the learned men on lecture platforms saying that what the Church needs is more and more activity, or if they heard certain counselors discouraging young girls from "wasting their lives as ivory-tower contemplatives", they would not understand. For these people are educated by misery to a certain kind of spiritual knowledge which the sheltered may not always attain. The instinct of near-despair brings them to the compassionate Christ of the Gospel or to those who live by His Gospel. And we love them and compassionate them as He does. To me, one of the surest signs of the vigor of the enclosed contemplative life in modern times is the way sinners and outcasts beat an unfailing path to its doors, just as others like them once came to "the Friend of publicans and sinners".

We grow so close to the Christ of the Gospel that our own souls soak up something of His wisdom, His gentleness, His humor, and His sorrow. We come to fathom the human depths of His tenderness and to suspect the divine, infinite depths. One particularly shattering consequence of the Incarnation was that it made the Godhead vulnerable. It would change the dull and faceless prayers we so often toss God's way if we remembered that mystery of vulnerability and let our lives be refashioned by it. It is true that the glorified humanity of Christ no longer suffers, but in the echoing timelessness of His divine Love, our niggardly half-measures were all woven into the thorny crown He wore in the year 33.

No man was ever so exquisitely modeled for suffering and for joy as the Man-God. Because His sacred Body was utterly perfect, He experienced the perfection of fatigue and hunger. Because no other mind ever reached the outposts of His divine intelligence, the stupidities and cruelties of men beat against His consciousness always with stony thuds. And because His sacred Heart held an infinite capacity for love, He vibrated to all forms of suffering like an incredibly perfect tuning fork catching a singing tone too rare for human ears.

That truth has its converse, too. Christ's human heart also vibrated with perfect delicacy to all forms of human joy. This utter tenderness is part of the Franciscan genius. It is what makes penance and sacrifice so attractive, for our hearts want to encompass all the sorrow and misery in the universe. We desire to make up in our bodies, as our Mother St. Clare did before us, those things that are wanting in the sufferings of Christ, to unstop the sin-corked heart of the world so that His saving blessings can flow in.

With this tender love of men comes a tender respect for all creatures favored by God with the miracle of life. The traditional Franciscan love of birds and beasts is a rich spiritual heritage from our Father St. Francis, and not the feather-headedness others sometimes suppose it to be. Too many persons think of St. Francis' affection for birds and animals as merely a charming trait in a good-natured fool. Ask ten different persons to tell you about St. Francis, and eight of them will most likely reply: "Oh, he talked to birds and patted rabbits on the head. A very good sort of fellow—not at all practical, of course, but frightfully generous to the poor."

Our holy Father Francis was the most practical man since the God-Man. He loved small creatures because their life was from God and spoke of divine goodness. What God thought worth creating, Francis and Clare thought worth respecting. And the animals responded to this marvelous love by forgetting their timidity or enmity with man and remembering the days in Eden when their forebears had lived with the first lord and lady of creation in mutual respect and a love that knew no fear. God's first plans for the fellowship of men and beasts seemed to fall back into their original lines when St. Francis walked the earth.

The Christ Who drove the cattle out of the vestibule of the temple, but "carried out the little doves in their cages", must be pleased to see the abbess in Roswell diligently washing the bugs out of a tiny stray kitten's fur while all the nuns leave their recreation sewing to assist at the important function.

The cats in the Roswell cloister realize they are creatures respected; and while it is true that they impose on the nuns outrageously, they do have their redeeming traits. Henna-furred Gran is shamefully unmortified about her food, but often piously attends the night Office, meowing her psalms with great feline fervor under the choir windows. Boloney, on the other hand, is not much for church services, but good-naturedly eats the weird pancakes Sister Anne concocts for the cats out of odd scraps of squash and mush.

All the monastic fowl and creatures small furnished us with a moving pageantry on the Feast of our holy Father

St. Francis last October 4, when we trooped out of the choir at sundown to sing our blessed Father's sublime poem, "The Canticle of the Sun", back in the vineyard. We faced the setting sun and began to sing. We had not got to the second strophe before a henna streak and a silver one flashed past us. Gran and Boloney settled themselves at Mother Abbess' feet, looking only slightly injured that they had not been called in time, and purred a joyous accompaniment to the canticle. The gander strode over with his accustomed dignity and stood at respectful attention without so much as a single honk until we had finished singing. Petty, our lone cow, gave St. Francis the highest tribute she has yet shown any man; she entirely suspended operations on her alfalfa while we sang! Little Pierro, our rabbit, became ecstatic with speed, apparently desiring to jump off the earth entirely and rest in St. Francis' stigmatized hands, which had so often cradled Pierro's ancestors.

To anyone who thinks that the Gospel cannot be taken quite literally today, I can only borrow Our Lord's words to St. Andrew: "Come and see!" Wild and sweet our Gospel rule of life may be, wild as the world considers voluntary penance, and sweet as the love of the Man in the Gospel. It is still the ancient Rule, which will always be completely modern. New religious Congregations are formed to fill special needs. Their rules and constitutions are framed for a present urgency, which may have disappeared a century hence. But even if there were not a single orphan in the world, not one captive to be ransomed or one sick man to nurse, or perhaps not even a solitary child to teach, the contemplative Orders would preserve their *raison d'être*. Freeze the whole world into a robust adulthood, and our Rule remains as practical as before. Just to "observe the holy Gospel of our Lord Jesus Christ" is the timeless Rule of St. Francis and St. Clare. As Father Philotheus Boehner, O.F.M., put it: Our Franciscan office in the Church is not so much to do anything as just to be.

"Seek ye first the kingdom of God and His justice, and all these things shall be added to you." So the Poor Clares, who live by the Gospel, never worry about things, knowing that things will be around when needed. This complete dependence on our divine Provider breathes the spirit of love and simple joy which so happily ensnared my heart during the first months of my monastic life. I still exult in it.

Our Lord told Margery Kempe, the anchoress of Lynn, that her enclosed life of union with Him gave Him the greatest satisfaction, and gave her "as great a right to be merry as any lady in the world". Poor Clares, too, live enclosed with Him and for Him. His Gospel is our Rule of life. And at the end of life, He will be there. Perhaps He will not send His Immaculate Mother and a company of virgins to escort us to Heaven, as He did when our holy Mother St. Clare came to die; but we trust to find His arms open for even the least of her daughters. So we do our penance and chant our Office and lose ourselves in the obscurity of a little cloister, and we are as merry as any ladies could ever be.

13 DOORS

Narrow is the gate and strait the way that leadeth to life . . . let us take heed, therefore, lest, having entered the way of the Lord, we should through our own fault, at any time depart from it.

—TESTAMENT OF ST. CLARE

People take doors for granted. And that is a great mistake. For doors are much more than movable panels in walls, swinging you from one place into another. They are always gateways, even when they are exits. All his life long, a man is walking steadily toward the gates of eternity, so he can never truly make an exit. He is forever going.

To me, doors are things of mystery and magnificence, opening on to new vistas of things which are each day a little less unseen, as the trek home to God brings us daily closer to the low door of Heaven.

Contemplative nuns might seem the least likely of persons to be absorbed by the thought of doors. A girl enters the cloister, and the great double enclosure doors are locked behind her. They are opened just once again, on her investiture day. Then their locks snap with finality, as far as she is concerned. In the world's way of reasoning, a Poor Clare is never going anywhere. Doors must be the least of her concerns. But it is not so. Precisely, if paradoxically, because she has shut one door behind her forever, an enclosed nun becomes preoccupied with the significance of doors. She could spell out her life story, as well as the history of her soul, by the doors of the monastery. Each door is a party to some climactic point in her life. And the doors know it.

When the monastic procession weaves its partnered way through the cloisters, I like to rehearse my life on the doors as we pass. They tell me the meaning of my life and remind me of where I am going. The procession passes the broad parlor door, which acts as sentinel to the stout enclosure doors. There, postulants kneel on trembling, silk-stockinged knees and beg in small, quick voices to be received into the monastic community, just as I knelt at the enclosure doors of the Chicago monastery, clutching the little paper the abbess had handed me through the parlor grille.

"Reverend Mother Abbess and dear Sisters, I beg you to receive me into your community", the paper said. That was what I wanted, all right. I yearned to shout it like thunder. At the least, I would couch the plea in ringing tones. But the big enclosure doors swung open, and I saw the nuns standing in two rows, heads slightly inclined and faces lost in the secrecy of veils. In one instant, I became completely dehydrated. After several heroic if unavailing attempts to swallow my suddenly nonexistent saliva, and hating myself for the uncertain rasp of my voice, I whispered hoarsely my plea to be admitted.

I nod respectfully to the broad-bosomed wisdom of the enclosure doors, which have heard the dry little voice of many a postulant after me and have closed compassionately upon her, waiting somewhat impatiently to open again on the day of her investiture a year later, when she is a beautiful bride of the Lord Jesus. That day, a satin cushion will be placed at the enclosure doors, and the young bride returning from the High Mass of her betrothals will kneel upon it and ask the Archbishop to "bless her entrance". This is the real entrance day, and her voice will not be uncertain then. My own did not thunder, but I remember that I heard a thousand bells ringing and ringing as I knelt on the small satin cushion.

The enclosure doors reached out for me like arms, and then they closed on my mother and my sister and the maze of dear faces, not cruelly but with loving comforting. "We will keep her safe for you forever", the big enclosure doors said to my mother, whose life of quiet sacrifice had taught me so much of things I would need to practice in the cloister, and to Mary, my lovely sister, who by any human scale of reasoning was so much finer material for the service of our Lord than I. "This is the daughter about whom you need never worry, and we will guard this child who can never grow away from you because her life and her love are sealed here in God." That is what the heavy enclosure doors whisper, year after year, to mothers and fathers, as they close behind eager young Poor Clare brides.

The procession returning to the choir from the refectory passes the vestibule leading to the novitiate, and I bow my head a bit lower to hide my smile as I go on chanting the processional psalm, *"Miserere mei, Deus"*. That tall, broad door of the novitiate at the end of the little vestibule knows why I smile. We are partners in a vast love for the wide-eyed postulants and the demure little novices who hurry through that big door a hundred times a day. Its wood is sweet with young laughter and salt with the unshed tears of the enervating, crawling nostalgia that gets little potential Poor Clares by the throats one time or another.

Often postulants are frightened of homesickness. They make a brave gesture of breaking clean with the world and all the persons and things in it as far as personal associations are concerned. And what happens? Instead of sweetness swimming in their souls and a warm glow encircling their hearts, they feel an icy fist jammed down their throats and a sickening sensation in the pits of their stomachs! Suddenly they want their mothers, their fathers, their friends, their books, their accustomed food, their independence. And the desire terrifies them. Surely it means they have no vocation.

Each postulant is sure that no one else who persevered could ever have felt like this. And each professed nun, noting the drooping mouth and misty eyes of some little black-skirted newcomer, remembers her own homesickness and compassionates the small sufferer. One of my postulant days, when the boulder in my throat was absolutely immovable, our wise Novice Mistress said casually: "It wouldn't be much of a compliment to your family and friends if you didn't miss them." I thought she must be endowed with the discerning of spirits or the reading of hearts like the great mystics; and I was properly impressed, even astounded. It never occurred to me that my drowned-cat expression could not possibly baffle anyone!

And that did it. The idea that it was perfectly natural and wholesome to miss your family and your friends and your former interests had simply never occurred to me, as it never occurs to any other postulant. I glance down the double file of nuns to the postulants. They look very small and dear. And then another smile stretches across my rush of tenderness for this year's little monastic beginners, as I reflect that their smallness of stature will spare them the dark moments I had just before my investiture as a novice.

I knew that Sister Teresa habitually communed with her own soul while fitting postulants for their first habit. I knew it because the communings were faintly audible. "Right shoulder is higher than the left . . . yes, yes . . . too bad . . . habit never will hang right." Sister Teresa was very short, and it was entirely appropriate that I was being fitted in the month of May. My tall thinness made such a perfect maypole for the quick dances she executed around me, a pin in her mouth and scissors in her hand, to the tune of that hum about my unfortunate right shoulder.

Then one day Sister Teresa looked up into my eyes, interrupting both dance and hum. Her face clouded. And as she resumed her whirling, the hum buzzed to a dark new strain: "Tall, tall . . . takes a lot of serge." I hung my

head in sorrow, wondering vaguely whether the community could really afford to keep me. And I sympa-
thized deeply with Sister Teresa's distress of soul that the
first postulants in Roswell were taller still. Kathleen and
Rosemary, too, had to suffer the chiding hum: "A lot of
serge . . . my oh my . . . too bad." Eleanor and Joan are a
distinct joy to Sister Teresa. Lovely postulants. Fine girls.
So small. I return to the strains of the *Miserere*, regretting
my lapse into reverie. "A contrite and humble heart Thou
wilt not despise, O God."

The door of the novitiate opens and closes for five
years of a young contemplative's life, until the day she
makes her perpetual vows. Then the door hears some
strange tunes. There is a party for the newly professed
Poor Clare, and the old door, whose varnish has glowed
with the cadences of Gregorian chant at many a practice
and vibrated to budding organists making their way
through the intricacies of model accompaniments, now
shivers under the shouted strains of "Oh, she's a jolly
good fellow, she's a jolly good fellow, she's a jolly good
fel-el-low, as nobody can deny!" The postulants and
novices yell it with boundless enthusiasm. The Novice
Mistress and the abbess join in sedately. And the young
nun for whom they are singing feels a warm sting under
her eyelids. Her real life in the community is beginning
now; but something tender and April-lovely is ending,
too. The novitiate door closes behind her understand-
ingly. That door deserves a saluting smile when we pass
it in procession.

Just down the cloister from the novitiate are the

handsome double doors of the chapter room. They are the sounding boards for some of the greatest moments in a nun's life. They know their dignity, and have a certain look of aloofness from the homelier details of living. After all, these are the doors that caught the abbess' voice and resounded her words: "For the greater honor and glory of God, the ever Blessed and Immaculate Virgin Mary, St. Joseph, our holy Father St. Francis, our holy Mother St. Clare and all the saints, and for the salvation and greater sanctification of your soul, your holy Profession will take place on the seventeenth day of September, the Feast of the sacred Stigmata of our holy Father St. Francis." And then the doors distinctly heard a young novice's heart exult in that great bound which only a consecrated virgin's heart can make when the banns of her wedding are cried.

These satiny doors have watched the abbess place silver wreaths on the heads of Poor Clare jubilarians. They have listened to nervous new novices and tremulous-voiced ancients declare the sorry little histories of their faults and shortcomings. And the doors have strained a bit on their hinges to catch Mother Abbess' gentle admonitions to her beloved offenders.

But the chapter room doors can unbend and be as merry as the novitiate door on occasion. During Christmas week they grow roguish under the encouragement of a spray of red ribbon and ornamental snowballs, and they swing exuberantly wide when the chapter room ceases to be a chapter room and becomes an auditorium for the Christmas songfest. The nuns troop in and gather

around the little organ, which I try to make sound like
the great organ in the choir. Sister Colette's chin rests on
her violin, and some of the novices bring their flutes.
And we sing and sing the ancient carols until the garlands over the chapter room altar shiver in appreciation,
and the dignified doors forget the confessions and admonitions they have heard. For it is Christmas, and each
nun will swear to it that there is no fault at all in any of
her Sisters, and the abbess flings the duty of correcting
down some back street of her mind. The Lord He is
small and very dear, and His love is the only reality in the
monastic Bethlehem. All these things I read in the grain
of the chapter room doors. The procession moves down
the last cloister with the sureness of those whose goal is
in view. The wide doors of the choir open like the arms
of the God they enclose. And I spell out the beginning
and purpose of my life upon them as surely as I see
the end of my life written unequivocally on their solid
panels.

These are the doors that lead to the wellspring of a
Poor Clare's life, the Tabernacle. They are the most
beautiful doors in the monastery because they are God's
inner gates, running with Office chants like rivers of
wine. They have heard the great organ flute out the
pastoral tunes of Christ's Birth and listened to it thunder
the soul-shaking glory of His Resurrection. They have
closed on the secret griefs of nuns stealing in for a private call on the Lord, Who knows what searing interior
trials He reserves for the souls of His contemplatives.
Only they are party to the untranslatable desolation of

soul by which God purifies His own and empties their
hearts and souls so that they are fit to bear the world and
all its griefs together. The joy of the enclosed contemplative life is stout fibered and enduring precisely because its roots reach down deep into the rich soil of
willing suffering. The choir doors are the binding on the
diary of each nun's soul.

And as the procession walks the broad boulevard of
the choir to genuflect before the altar, we come to the
small doors that declare their supreme importance by the
little padlocks spread across them like medallions. They
have four panels, and each panel signifies something epic
in a Poor Clare's life. Each morning, Sister Amata un-
locks one panel so that the Sacramental Jesus may come
to each member of the community in Holy Communion. Once a month she opens the cross-barred panel,
where a Franciscan friar sits to tell his cloistered Franciscan Sisters of God and of the ways to love Him more.

Next month, Sister Dolores will make her final vows.
Then they will unlock two panels of the grate doors for
her, so that her mother and father will see her happy face
as they listen to the voice of their child promising to be
completely God's forever and for all eternity.

I look meditatively at two lower panels, which I have
seen unlocked only once, when Archbishop Byrne and
his entourage entered the choir on the day of the dedication of the new chapel and monastery. One day they
will be opened for me. It will be the day when my coffin
is placed before the grate, and people will file by to look
at my dead face. I hope they will say what people always

say when they look upon a dead Poor Clare. "How happy she looks, how peaceful!" The Franciscan friars will come through those doors after my Requiem Mass and escort me to the little cemetery in the cloister garden. My Sisters will sing: "May the angels conduct you into Paradise." And afterward they will have a festive dinner in my honor, and there will be recreation all afternoon because I have achieved my goal and finished my course. I hope they will miss me a little; I know they will envy me. And I will sleep in the little cemetery where my Sisters will come to visit me after they have said the Stations of the Cross under the trees. They will spread benedictions of holy water over my grave and ask my Spouse to grant me eternal rest.

There is the end of my life, spread like a banner across the four-paneled grate. It is good to see it, each time I enter the choir.

And now it is Advent. Wreaths of redwood and fir form their own Advent O's against the doors. We leave the choir and pass under the life-sized image of our Lady of Guadalupe which the Trappist monks in Pecos gave us, and we remark with satisfaction how lightly she balances on her lovely redwood wreath. We ask her to bless their new foundation in Oregon, which is also named for her. Eleanor and Joan lead the procession, heads demurely bent over their suffrage books until the spray of snowballs at the chapter room doors proves too much for them. The two black-veiled heads turn for a quick, delicious glance, and then jerk back to book and psalm. Branches of fir are piled high in the novitiate vestibule, and I draw in the clean fragrance of them in a breath so long it has come up from my bare toes and will return to them. The glass-paneled door of the community room is discreetly curtained, because wonderful and mysterious things are being wrought in there by Mother Vicaress.

We come into the refectory, and Sister Catherine is no longer tired from hours on a ladder when she hears the "ah!" of the nuns sigh through the chant of the *Miserere*. We bow to the crucifix from Oberammergau, and there is a star above it. Heavy green garlands loop their way down the bare white walls of the refectory, and a red wreath swings from the window. And, oh, wonderful to tell!—three tiny velvet bears are sliding down the wire tail of the big refectory telechron! The postulants' eyes are enormous. And the chaste and lovely Beuron Crib takes possession of the refectory and of us.

The monastery is on tiptoe. The cloisters are full of whispers and rumors. "All things are ready", we declared in the antiphon at Lauds this morning. Yet postulants, novices, and nuns race about the monastery as though nothing at all were ready! And I draw my conviction about me like a warm mantle that Advent is the season of contemplatives. Hidden away from the glare and noise of worldly living, we are enclosed in the womb of holy Church. This season of quiet and waiting and utter trust is the season our lives never quit. I walk down the cloisters, and my heart moves to a single tune: Lord, it is good, so good to be here!

Today is the day before Christmas Eve, and our joy stirs within us and dilates our throats. "*Prope est jam*

Dominus"—"the Lord is already near." See what a small, poor, hidden Lord He is Who lay unknown in Bethlehem, but held the whole world in His beating human heart. This is our season.

GLOSSARY

OF MONASTIC TERMS

BOOK OF SUFFRAGES—a book of particular prayers for particular needs and for our benefactors..

CANONICAL HOURS—the divisions of the Divine Office: Matins, Lauds, Terce, Sext, None, Vespers, and Compline.

CELL—a nun's bedroom.

CHAPTER—the formal assemblage of the professed nuns either for the confession of public faults or for taking a canonical voting on postulants and novices.

CHOIR—that part of the chapel which is inside the enclosure.

COLLATION—a light repast, taken in the evening.

ENCLOSURE VEIL—a very long, thin veil which partially covered the face and was always worn outside the enclosure or at the parlor or choir grille. This is no longer worn.

EXTERN SISTERS—Sisters who do not make a vow of enclosure, and attend to the outside business of the monastery. We no longer have extern Sisters.

FRANCISCAN CROWN—a "Rosary" of seven decades, each mystery corresponding to one of the seven joys of our Lady, recited at least once daily by Franciscans.

GRATE OR GRILLE—the opening in the church through which the nuns receive Holy Communion, are given conferences, etc.; or the one in the parlor through which they visit their relatives.

HEBDOMADARIA—the nun, appointed for one week, who officiates at the Divine Office for that period, gives the blessings at table, and leads all the prayers.

PORTRESS—the nun appointed to transact the monastery business at the turn or grille.

STALL—a nun's place in the choir, consisting of a desk and a bench.

THE TURN—a revolving cabinet-like affair through which articles are given in from outside, or passed outside from the cloister.

VERSICULAR—the nun, appointed for one week, who intones the antiphons and psalms of the Divine Office at each hour.

VICARESS—the second superior, assistant to the abbess.